The Art of Authentic Friendship

Judy Dippel &
Debra Whiting Alexander, Ph.D.

Mobile, Alabama

The Art of Authentic Friendship
by Judy Dippel and Debra Whiting Alexander

ISBN 978-1-58169-283-9
For Worldwide Distribution
Printed in the U.S.A.

Evergreen Press
P.O. Box 191540 • Mobile, AL 36619
800-367-8203

Table of Contents

DEDICATION

To our friends…

past,

present,

and future.

ACKNOWLEDGMENTS

We extend our sincere gratitude to all the women who responded to our survey and interviews in such a real and transparent manner. Their contributions of written materials, wisdom, hurt, and humor were invaluable experiences for us to draw from—they are living proof of the value of women's friendships.

To our publisher, Evergreen Press, for believing in the message of our book, and to our editors—Brian, Jeff, and Kathy Banashak—for countless hours spent and your ability to wade through two authors' efforts and opinions. It's been a pleasure.

Special thanks to Kathryn Wilson for valuable feedback received as we began writing, and permission to include her poem, "Friends I've Found" in our manuscript.

From Judy:

Thanks to my husband, Mark—my best friend, who brings perspective and balance to my spurts of estrogen, consistently encouraging as my writing drafts come to life on the written page.

And Debra—I'm so glad you came first in the phone book.

From Debra:

The bond I share with lifelong friends has been nothing short of inspiring. A number of you have been especially helpful to me while writing this book. I am boundlessly grateful to: Deborah Heal, Susan Jorgensen, Corinne Marie, Tita Evans-Santini, Maureen Thrash, Rhoda Weber, and Kathryn Wilson. Better friends do not exist.

My continuing affection and appreciation go to my husband, Bob, and daughter, Katelyn. Their love lets me know how fortunate I am.

To my co-author of this book, and newfound friend, Judy. This book took over our lives so fast I still owe you lunch!

Finally, my thanks go to God, for allowing me the privilege to write.

PREFACE

From Judy:

Like an adventurous road trip with a new girlfriend, writing this book brought unexpected curves and important discoveries. And, it's been quite a ride.

Initially, I believed writing a book about women and friendship would be a breeze. Influenced by an array of wonderful friends whom I have known over the years, my passion and vision for this book seemed clear. But as life would have it, some of my lifelong friendships suddenly got "all shook up."

I never imagined anything could threaten the unwavering, indisputable bonds I shared with my friends. But I was wrong. My idealistic bubble burst with the hurt and challenges I faced in these relationships. I was shocked, confused, and left wondering, "what happened?" Circumstances with these few close friends left me feeling inadequate to write on this important topic. Consequently, my initial draft for a book sat untouched to collect dust for two years.

I alternately raged and rested in God as I did some heavy soul-searching, trying to understand what was happening with these particular friends. Women are all about relationships, and not one of us is perfect. I frequently and glibly reminded myself, "It's not our fault that we have problems—God's well aware of our frailties, since He made us this way." But for a season, I grieved and wept, self-condemned and prayed. Gratefully, clarity of heart and mind slowly returned.

With the passage of time, and after continued seeking of God's counsel, I began to tackle this writing project again. This time I knew the message of this book must look and feel very different. However, I still struggled with how to write about and celebrate the importance of women's friendships, while several of my own were flailing. I decided to seek out a practicing therapist to write this book with me—an expert who could offer sound strategies and professional insights to this topic. I went to the yellow pages and phoned Debra.

From Debra:

When Judy called me at home one morning and pitched her desire to author a book about friendship, I told myself the same thing I had been telling everyone: "I'm not writing any more non-fiction." I was done for the simple reason that I felt I had already written about the issues for which I held the most passion. My brain was harvested, all knowledge extracted, and now only fictitious, make-believe characters roamed inside my head for my first novel.

However, Judy was persistent, so I rehearsed my "I'm too busy to work with you" speech and spoke to her again. And it was true. Between a full-time practice, teaching, speaking engagements, and living with a teenager and an adult male, this statement was an accurate enough description of my life.

Still, I hated to say no. I decided the least I could do was encourage Judy and share my own experiences in the world of publishing. And besides, she offered to buy me lunch at a restaurant I liked.

I assumed Judy called me because she knew I was an author and liked all the books I'd written. We laugh now, knowing she called me because I happened to be under the A's in the phone book listings. In other words, she had never heard of me. God has a way of keeping us humble and laughing, but He can also connect us to people at just the right times.

It's one thing to talk easily to someone on the phone, but to meet a stranger in person can be another thing. When Judy and I met, our lunch date transformed instantaneously into a friendship. We talked for hours, and I was surprised at how easily we connected and "hit it off," especially when we began discussing the topic of women's friendships.

So I was wrong. Maybe there was one more non-fiction project I would enjoy tackling. But the truth is, my motivation initially was less about writing and more about recognizing a new friend.

From both of us:

And so, our collaboration on this book began. Our first lunch was a marathon; because of course, no one can "do lunch" like two women, especially when they're new friends. We talked marriage, children, menopause, growing up, parents, laughter, fun, and food—all the while discussing careers, and the writing and vision for this book. During our first few meetings, we moved rapidly through the stages of friendship, well past the superficial. Month after month, we eagerly worked together to bring the best both of us has to offer, writing a book that meshed our strengths and weaknesses.

Meaningful relationships for both of us are the first priority: our relationship with God, family, and a variety of friends. As baby-boomers entering mid-life, we feel passionate about the importance of, and need for, solid friendships. In doing so, we learned it is necessary to look at actions and reactions that help or hinder success in these relationships.

To be an authentic friend, you must embrace the freedom of being authentic yourself, just as God intends you to be. This book will help lead you through difficult times when you are left feeling less than content or authentic in your friendships. It is our prayer that as you seek more of God in the process, you will be inspired and equipped to find the peaceful, healthy solutions that will lay within your reach. Like us, we trust you will enjoy the ride and learn from many personal discoveries along the way.

In friendship,
—Judy and Debra

INTRODUCTION

Dozens of books have been written that extol the beauty and joy of women's friendships. Most of them celebrate and delight in all the qualities that make ideal or perfect friends. This is not one of those books.

While we appreciate the primary messages found in other books, we know there's a lot about women's relationships that isn't easy. Friendships can change fast; sometimes they unravel in unpredictable and painful ways. T*he Art of Authentic Friendship: Real Women, Real Challenges, Real Solutions* is a book not only about the problems that put valued friendships to the test but also their solutions.

We surveyed and interviewed women between the ages of thirty and eighty-five for this project. We asked them to list and describe the top ten challenges they've faced with women friends and how they handled each situation. Women told us firsthand how difficult it can be to cope with broken or lost friendships. In fact, women from all walks of life confirmed to us the fact that friendship is not a trivial subject. It's a highly charged emotional one, especially when things go wrong.

Friends represent roots going straight to the heart and reflect who a woman is and what is important to her. When friendships are interrupted by difficult times, even temporarily, women clamor for answers and ways to cope. Bridget (age 41) said, "I was at a complete loss when my friend betrayed my trust. I was so stunned by her actions that I could barely speak to her again."

Individuals who responded to our questionnaires and interviews shared their deepest thoughts and feelings. They revealed a rich reservoir of wisdom and humor from which to draw. Women described how difficult it was to cope with the pain and stress that broken relationships leave in their wake. In some cases they shared journal entries with us, and even correspondence written to and from friends. The participants involved in our research came from all walks of life. Even though this was not a scientific study, those who participated represented a variety of professional and cultural backgrounds. Not all the women with whom we spoke or surveyed shared our Christian faith. But then, not all our friends do either.

Despite the range of friendship challenges they experienced, many women explained that friendships are still something they cannot do without. They said they function better and handle the stress and trials of life more effectively when they can share their daily struggles with someone else. When friendships were threatened by adversity, women said they suffered miserably. As one 40-year-old woman stated, "My world fell apart when an important friendship ended. It was devastating to me. I depended on her, and part of my life has never been the same since."

Friendship is good for women when relationships are positive and mutually satisfying. Research confirms that friendship even improves women's physical health. Having close friends can counteract the effects of stress and reduce the risk of disease. Women live longer and better in the company of their friends. Whether high levels of stress come from work or relationships, women survive these challenges more easily with confidants. Women who vent and bond with friends who listen and empathize are practicing a natural form of effective stress management. Researchers have concluded that not having close friends or confidants is as detrimental to health as smoking or carrying extra weight (Nurses' Health Study, Harvard Medical School; reported in timeforbalance.com, "Women's Friendships Vital to Health," the Louden Network, Inc., 2004).

Friendships that aren't functioning well can seriously impact women's lives and generate intense anguish. In short, when friendships are jeopardized, women suffer. Whether friendship challenges are mild or toxic, emotional battle wounds can scar the psyche and change the course of one's life. We want to help change that.

The Art of Authentic Friendship offers solutions to the most pressing issues that put women's relationships at risk today. Regardless of how much women need each other, in today's time-demanding stressful culture, it's a challenge for most to make friendship a priority. Others experience obstacles or conflicts that result in difficult or lost friendships. Many women harbor unhealthy amounts of anger and resentment from frustrating past experiences. Some women may not be willing to accept or forgive their friends, and as a result, they miss opportunities for lasting connections with one another. When left unchecked, problems with jealousy and competitiveness can grow like cancer in relationships. So can envy and unrealistic expectations. We learned that emotional aggression happens as frequently in Christian friendships as in non-Christian ones and can be extremely hard to reconcile.

High maintenance or "needy" friends can also take a toll on a person's well-being. Women may ruminate and suffer in silence as they face harrowing challenges with friends. Many don't know how to help those living through domestic violence and addiction, or serious mental health issues. There are other challenges as well—difficulties that drive women to lose friendships entirely or lose themselves within a friendship. Others have grieved the loss of friends who have died. *The Art of Authentic Friendship* is designed to help you face all these struggles and more.

There is an art to making and keeping friends, and there

is an art to surviving some of them too. Despite the potential benefits of relationship counseling, few women seek therapy to improve friendships. *The Art of Authentic Friendship* contains the therapeutic tools and counseling advice needed to improve and even prevent painful experiences with friends. It's designed to instruct and inspire while reassuring women they are never alone in whatever challenges they face. Women will gain knowledge through God's Word—blending faith with therapeutic tools. They will have the opportunity to apply practical solutions specifically designed to help repair and sustain meaningful, close friendships.

The Art of Authentic Friendship is divided into two parts. Part One, *Friendship Challenges and Solutions*, contains six chapters representing the top challenges women face: Time, Obstacles, Anguish, Healthy Choices, You, and Relationships.

Each chapter introduces the reader to critical issues with which women said they wanted help. The challenges addressed are supported by true stories and quotes we gathered. A variety of topics related to each challenge are explored as well. The following sections are found in each chapter:

The *Solution* section of each chaper offers professional insight through counseling advice and guidelines. These hands-on strategies are offered to instruct and encourage women. The action steps provided will help minimize and prevent long-term difficulties each friendship challenge can produce. Readers will learn coping skills and gain practice in effective communication and problem solving.

"When to Seek Further Help" is a section for readers in need of more help than one book can provide. Helplines and resource numbers are also listed in the back of the book.

Soul Solutions recognizes the ultimate guide for building

and sustaining healthy relationships is found in Scripture. Through God's Word and grace, wounds can be healed from a disappointing or hurtful friendship. In this section, scriptures and a prayer guide are offered to encourage and inspire women to seek God and His solutions in whatever concerns them.

Friend-to-Friend Activities can be found at the end of each chapter. These activities can help women take proactive steps towards creating positive friendships. Not only are they designed to be interesting and fun, they will give readers creative ideas for enriching or rekindling important relationships. Most importantly, they are designed to bring friends closer and strengthen bonds.

Part Two, *Friendship and Beyond,* contains three brief chapters which address the universal, yet critical issues regarding: Finding Friends, Growing a Relationship with God, and Leaving a Legacy of Friendship. Not everyone feels they have the opportunities to find friends, or the necessary social skills to form friendships. Lack of confidence and shyness may contribute to this challenge. Our book also addresses the importance of growing a relationship with God, the ultimate role model for experiencing healthy and lasting friendships. We appreciate that each person's faith journey is different, yet we know how critical it is to include the spiritual foundation God provides equally to all. The final chapter encourages women to leave a legacy and tradition of friendship behind them.

Friendships are nearly as important as food, rest, and exercise. Finding solutions to the challenges women face is too important to neglect. Life can be expanded and affirmed in immeasurable ways by friendships that remain beneficial for the heart, mind, body, and soul. Positive self-worth and personal growth are inspired by healthy friendships. Simply put, friends are good for women! In a culture that is increasingly complex and confusing, true friends—the soul mates in women's lives—are lifelines to overall well-being.

To keep a woman's most important friendships intact and healthy, we challenge readers to use this book to discover new ways to relate to others and resolve difficulties with them both now and in the future. From there, it is our sincere hope that a legacy of friendship will be steadily built—friend-to-friend—without interruption.

PART ONE:

FRIENDSHIP CHALLENGES AND SOLUTIONS

Chapter 1

Time

> I certainly need time with my women friends, but with their busy lives and my busy life, it's very difficult to just be together, relax, and let friend-stuff happen. As women, we expect so much of ourselves in today's world. We wear so many different hats, and have so many responsibilities. I honestly think the number one challenge we all face is finding time for each other. *—Marianne (age 48)*

Today, this very moment, will never happen again. Living life in a fast-paced society is a constant reminder that minutes steal away. Days come and go, and weeks seem to fly by. Months are torn from the calendar, and holidays blend quickly from one to another. Time presses forward, unyielding. To-do lists and appointments fill up day planners with little or no time scheduled in for meaningful relationships. Trying to manage time is the ultimate stressor and finding time to be with friends is indeed the greatest challenge women face.

Living a productive and accomplished life is part of God's plan, and successful women deserve to be celebrated. In reality there is no way around the hectic days of family life or a time-demanding job or career. The many responsibilities women hold and *want* to hold help give life special meaning and purpose. However, it's also part of God's plan for women to benefit from the companionship of friends. Experiencing support from other women and having fun with them adds a dimension to life that is priceless.

The ability to find delight in each day and in the simplicity of the moment helps foster attitudes that value the importance of friendship. It's no secret that women's relationships add satisfaction and bring balance and well-being to life. Secure and caring friendships with other women are one of the most effective ways you nurture yourself, second only to time spent with God.

Sometimes women form an instant bond, but most often they require time and repeated opportunities to get to know each other. Plainly, friends need frequent time together that is intentional and planned. Without creating opportunity, significant friendships may remain simple passing acquaintances. Elizabeth (age 53) described it this way: "Acquaintances are the pedestrians in life. They walk in and out, back and forth, and stroll around your life; but they're always just passing through. They're not here to stay."

Social contacts are nice, but a true friend is life-changing. Sandy (age 46) shared: "Friends are like iron sharpening iron. My genuine friends strengthen, expand, and inspire my life, not so much by what they do for me, but by what they motivate me to do and be." Contemporary society with all its demands does not alter the fact that women are created for connection to one another. As Elizabeth concluded, "The connection I feel with true friends is profound; it means I am not alone."

In Generations Past

When I was a young woman, we lived out on the farm. We woke early, and like women today, we rarely stopped. The chores back then were especially

> physical and time-consuming. Hard! Tending children in addition to laundry, dishes, ironing, sweeping, baking, cooking, gardening, sewing, and canning kept us busy every day. Women's hands were never idle. Good things came from our hard work. Whether we were plucking chickens, quilting, or gardening, we did these things together. This was our time to talk, although in those days I kept a lot more feelings to myself than women do today. But it was my social club, because I had few other places to meet women friends. *—Mabel (age 85)*

Historically women's lives offered less diversions and distractions. This resulted in a slower pace that some might even call mundane by today's standards. Though hard-working as they set about their daily routines, women still had opportunities to connect and bond with one another. Women gathered to work on common interests or chores that were done out of necessity. Their way of life built in the priority and time to have simple, meaningful conversation. There weren't cell phones or the Internet, so on any given day visitors and friends were a welcome highlight. The same was true for many neighborhoods in the 1950s and 60s.

Claudine (age 79) remembers:

> In the 50s life was slower. In our neighborhood, most women stayed home. We had only one car (my husband drove it to work). This kept me at the house most days. Neighborhood friends just dropped in; they didn't call first or need an invitation, because we needed each other for our social life. Routinely, we sat and visited over coffee in the morning or a Pepsi in the afternoon. It put us behind, but we had all day to catch up. We shared recipes, housekeeping

> tips, family and kid problems, jokes and dreams. I miss these kinds of visits. Yesterday, I put up my Christmas tree and at the mailbox a neighbor said, "Your tree looks so nice through the window." I appreciated her comment, but I miss the days when the Christmas tree going up was a signal for an impromptu get-together, exchange of home-baked goodies, and visiting. I have nice neighbors, but I cannot imagine one knocking on my door to see my tree. They are too busy.

Today's world looks and feels much different, but women still have a fundamental need for one another. In a world rapidly changing and sometimes isolating, moving past the superficial to really get to know someone isn't always easy. Even though access to one another seems easier, technology has both connected and disconnected our relationships. Although it's different today than in generations past, bonding together like women used to do in the "old days" is still possible.

Solutions

What steps can be taken to improve or increase the amount of quality time you spend with friends? This may seem like an overwhelming challenge, but it can also be exciting to make new changes in your life. The solution to finding time with friends begins by examining your awareness about priorities you set and the importance you give them.

Make Friends a Priority

The fact you are reading this book means friendship is already something you value. You know having enough time with friends is critical. The hours you share together serve a dual purpose. To your friend you affirm the importance of the relationship; to yourself you confirm the importance of your need of friends for personal well-being. You both win when you place time with friends high on the list of your priorities.

Meet Tita. She is a fifty-three-year-old Mexican-American woman who thrives within a wide circle of friends. For Tita, friends have always taken precedence and always will. Making time for them is a non-negotiable choice she made a long time ago. People ask Tita all the time, "How do you find time for so many friends?" Being an extrovert helps, but she's also happy and deeply expressive. Anywhere you go, Tita knows someone. To watch her greet people, you would think every person she embraced was her long lost, dearest friend. Here's what she said about making friends a priority:

> For as long as I can remember, I've valued my friends; I make time for them. It's always been a priority. It's not work; it comes naturally. I need relationships in my life, and I'm loyal to friends. It's a value, and it's at the core of who I am. I was a sad, lonely, and shy child. Coming to the United States as a young girl, I didn't know the language or even understand the conveniences of indoor plumbing. I experienced culture shock, violence, and addiction in my home, but I was grateful for the water that poured out of our faucets and the strong roof over our head. My gratitude grew for every non-violent, non-addicted, gentle person who came into my life. It's hard to sort out life at any age, but at every age I've used friends as a sounding board. If I'm seeing all "red" they help me see "blue." It's the yin and yang thing, equilibrium and balance.

> I take my friends with me wherever I go, and I use their intellect, wisdom and humor to help me respond in situations that are new to me. Don't ask me why it's a priority; that seems like a silly question! Why is it a priority to breathe? It's part of my need to live. Life is relationships for me. If you aren't spending time with friends, you aren't living. Yes, time is precious, and everyone's busy. So what? I lost a friend a couple years ago to a brain aneurysm, and I still find time to be with her. Yeah, once every season, I run to her grave, and I still spend time with her. I carry her so vividly in my mind that I know exactly what she would say to me and how she would say it. I know that because we knew each other inside and out. That happened because of the value we placed on our time together. I loved her then and still love her now. Had we not made time for one another, a part of me would not be who I am today.

When time together is this powerful, it's easy to make friends a priority. If you stop and reflect on what friends contribute to your own life, you recognize what you stand to lose without them. Many women have lost friends to death, but even more have lost friends to the black hole of hurried lives. As the *Soul Care Bible* states: "At the end of our life, many of us will realize that we have spent most of our time on what matters least, and the least time on those things that matter most" (p. 423, 2005)

Every day you have decisions to make. Begin by spending time with friends who matter most to you. When your days are nearing their end, the life choices you've made may mean the difference between remorse and contentment.

Practice Intentional Living

Regardless of your age or role in life, your world may be too busy. Daily commitments can crowd out the experiencing of true pleasure. Simple blessings are not intentionally disregarded, but busyness can easily drown them out. Many women live too many of their waking hours on a treadmill and have forgotten what true relaxation feels like. Without it, they may miss built-in opportunities for friendship. Learning to live in the present moment is another important step to finding time for relationships.

To allow your senses to awaken to and appreciate this very moment takes deliberate practice. Life's pressures can cause you to focus on what's to come next, rather than focusing on what's happening right now. Our culture has gotten into the habit of racing the clock. It's a society bent on achieving goals and endless "doing." All too often time for yourself or with friends is blurred in the rush or buried underneath a blanket of thoughts that rarely come up for air. The world pushes you to keep up with all the demands it imposes, and consequently, the beauty of each day or anything else around you is hardly noticed.

Even in the freedom of your home, it may be difficult to allow yourself to pause and quietly retreat into stillness. Scores of women are not able to stop long enough to give themselves license to do nothing for a time. Others say they either don't know how, or have forgotten to relax and enjoy life without feeling guilty or overburdened. They feel compelled to accomplish something at every point in their day.

When you lose the ability to slow down and simply have fun, you often lose your sense of spontaneity too. Learning to live in the moment can help you enjoy more time with friends. At the same time, friends can help you live spontaneously. No matter where you are, think of it as an "adult recess." Not only can life be more stimulating when it's unplanned, but it can sometimes be a treat not to arrange a thing. Just let life happen!

The habit of a hurried lifestyle has become a prestigious badge many women wear. It's often viewed as an acceptable and expected way of life. Slowing down and learning to live in the present moment means *you are living intentionally,* or you are practicing intentional living. In either case, it's key to making more time for friends.

Life is not always easy or fun, so seize every opportunity you have to make your days more enjoyable. The more you embrace time rather than race or resist it, the easier you'll be able to spend it in more satisfying ways. Begin with small steps and make gradual changes.

What you can do:

Are you living intentionally? Review the following points. Evaluate each strategy by placing a 1, 2, or 3 next to it. Use the following scale:

1 = I will do it today 2 = I will try to do it tomorrow
3 = I already do it

• *Focus on the present* and pay attention to your surroundings. Tune in to what you are doing this very minute. Use your senses: look, listen, smell, touch. Be mindful of right now. The world is ever-changing. A sense of mindfulness can inspire you to slow down and appreciate a more relaxing pace.

• *Pay attention to the people around you.* Smile and encourage those with whom you have contact. Make a habit of connecting with others in ways you enjoy too. Who can measure the effect? Kindness is contagious and makes you feel good about life.

• *Breathe.* It sounds trite, but taking slow, deep breaths

throughout the day is another way to ease the anxiety that can result from a stressful or hurried day. Slowly inhale through your nose. Breathe deeply as if inflating a balloon where your stomach sits just above your belly button. Exhale out your mouth even more slowly. As you exhale, think of a short word or phrase to say to yourself. Examples: peace, surrender, faith, calm, God is present, the Lord is my strength.

• *Take a personal time out every day.* Refresh yourself doing something you love. Listen to music, sing, play the piano, garden, enjoy a recreational activity, read, sew, take a bubble bath, have a pedicure, etc.

• *Maintain a sense of humor.* Spend plenty of time with friends who make you laugh and who think you're funny too. Entertain one another; it will brighten your day.

• *Cultivate a thankful heart.* "Count your blessings" is not just a catchphrase. Keep a gratitude journal and list what you are thankful for every day. Review these pages as reminders of what you have to appreciate.

• *Do one spontaneous thing every day*, no matter how small it seems. Fluctuate your morning routine, drive an alternate route, hop on your bike, visit a new store, take the kids to a different park, perk up your brown bag by coloring a picture on it—anything, just as long as you put intentional living into practice.

Time Management

Obviously, not all of life can be unplanned. Most women can't live in spur-of-the-moment situations on a regular basis. Additional strategies for making time for one another may be necessary. Learning to take control of your schedule, rather than letting it take control of you, is what time management is all about.

Remember, the goal is to spend time with people who bring out the best in you and are inspiring to be around. Consider making "appointments" with friends who may have busy routines each day too. View time with friends like essential engagements on your calendar. Making the commitment is important. You need support for the many ups and downs in life and the chance to let your hair down.

Nevertheless, adding social time can still be hard to add to your schedule. Sometimes it ends up adding more stress instead of decreasing it. Susan (age 50) said: "Scheduling time together is the biggest challenge I find with friends. We make more time for our children, spouse's or boyfriends, and work, than these deep nurturing relationships that often last longer than love relationships or a job . . . but how can we do it all? We end up feeling even more overwhelmed."

Many women say they feel like they're on-call to everyone in their lives. Friends often take a back seat only because they can. Family and career responsibilities often must come first, but resentment and frustration are likely to build when you don't give yourself some time off. The same is true with our tears too; we often reach a breaking point when we least expect it and begin crying over nothing. Fighting an uphill battle for every minute in a day depletes you of energy and leaves you weary and battle fatigued, but alternatives do exist.

Time is not the enemy, but your perspective about it might be. In fact, time is on your side when you learn how to effectively manage each day's hours. When scheduling conflicts arise, ask yourself these three critical questions:

1. If I were gone tomorrow, would anyone care that I did or did not do this?
2. Will time spent with friends be meaningful or helpful?
3. What is most important to me?

Time with friends does not have to detract from other important relationships. Small adjustments in how you carry out your days can make a significant difference. With effective time management, you really can have your cake and eat it too.

Tita continued her discussion about making room in her life for friends and spoke about managing her time:

> I am busy. In fact I am more than busy. I'm married, I have two teenage sons, and I live in a house that proves I live with two teenage sons and 15 of their best friends! Some days it's complete chaos, and cluttered, and noisy all the time. Everything turns loud the minute one of them opens the front door. And there are "boy things" everywhere ... dirty socks and pizza boxes and skateboards and CDs and sweatshirts full of sweat! And one day too soon, I will miss this craziness and crave to hear their loud voices and thundering feet crossing the kitchen floor to the refrigerator! I know that, so I accept it's always going to be a struggle to keep the house clean. It's okay. I let it go. I have a life to live too. I work two jobs, I am politically active, I'm an artist, and I always, always, always make time for my women friends.
>
> It's not that I'm super woman—far from it. It's just that I couldn't do all of what I do, or be all of who I am without my friends in my life. It's the best therapy in the world. I make it my priority. Because it is. You have to set dates to connect with friends. It's the best thing you will ever do for your schedule. You just do it. You make it first—every chance you get.

Much of stress is self-induced. Like Tita, individual attitude makes a difference. You can regain control of your time through choices that bring balance to life. Your decision to break old habits and create new ones may feel as good as a therapy session with your best friend.

What you can do:

How well are you managing your time? Review the following points. Evaluate each strategy by placing a 1, 2, or 3 next to it. Use the following scale:

1 = I will do it today 2 = I will try to do it tomorrow
3 = I already do it

• Imagine you have three extra hours a week. Make a wish list of how you would spend them. Challenge yourself to add at least one wish from your list to your schedule within the next two weeks.

• Spend more time doing what is important to you. Frequently ask yourself, "Is this really what I want to be doing right now?"

• Assess how your time is spent. Take your monthly calendar and highlight important dates and events with different colored pens. These might include job related duties, appointments, "musts" with kids, alone time with spouse, time for yourself, recreation, time with friends, etc. Do you have a rainbow of colors, or are some missing? Does this align with what you value most in your life?

• To free up more time for friends, let something go. You need to balance your time and commitments differently than you have in the past. Frequently remind yourself that your needs do matter. It's not selfish to cancel an unnecessary activity or add more fun to your schedule to bring balance to your life.

• Don't forget to keep your day planner or Palm Pilot

handy. Carry it with you at all times to help you protect whatever free time you can. If you don't do this already, stick it in your purse so you can check your schedule on the spot.

• Your friends are a valued investment, so invest valuably. Write one or more names with phone numbers at the top of your "to do" list. Remember, good friends are de-stressors and good for your health. Your tension will lesson as you look forward to dates scheduled with people important to you.

• Take turns scheduling dates and activities with friends on a regular basis.

• Break up unmanageable tasks into manageable chunks. By completing one small goal at a time, a large job becomes achievable and less overwhelming when completed over several days. For example, organize one small section of your desk or kitchen cabinet at a time. Simply de-clutter a room rather than deep clean it right away. Weed one small section of the yard and organize paper work before actually having to complete it. Prepare your desk for work before sitting down to do the work, and make a list of errands in the order you need them done before actually running them.

• Team up with a friend to accomplish a challenging task together. Your weakness may be her strength, and vice versa. It won't seem nearly as big, and you'll have fun while you're working. Reward yourselves when you're done.

• Make technology work for you. Let answering machines and e-mails do what they are designed to do—save your messages! Wait to respond when you're not distracted and when the time is convenient for you. Some women prefer to respond to all their messages at once. Others make the choice to take days off from technology altogether. Remember, if it's not a life or death situation, people can wait. You get to decide when and how you handle your own machines!

- If something on your schedule seems impossible, this may be a clue to make a change. For example, you may feel stretched thin volunteering in too many areas or putting in too much overtime at work or at home. Be creative and think outside the box. Learn to accept help and delegate to others, or simply accept the fact that's it's more than you're willing to do and give yourself permission to let it go.
- Balance your day, rather than juggle it. To balance is to control; to juggle is to risk dropping every ball you have in the air.
- Keep in mind the way you think about managing your time is a powerful way to change your perspective. You have more control than you realize.

As you begin to apply these suggestions to your life, remember it can take self-discipline and hard work to accomplish a "time management make-over." You need motivation to take action, so maintain a positive attitude and keep your goals simple to ensure success. Each time you reserve time for friends, the rewards will quickly follow.

No Time or No Interest?

It's not always easy to spend what little time you have with friends you're not that close to. It's okay to conserve your time for friends who matter most. When there's someone who meets a need in a way no one else can, don't hesitate to seek that friend out before others. For many of you, making this one change will have a huge impact on your time. You can be kind and still say no. If you feel obliged to spend time with people, remember that friendships don't grow well on a foundation of obligation or guilt.

The more honest you are with yourself, the more honest you can be with others. Being candid and real will save you time and energy in the long run.

Christians are called to love one another (see John 13:34) and to befriend those in need whenever possible. However, you can't be best friends with everyone. Give yourself permission to spend leisure time with women who truly satisfy your soul.

Even when you have plenty of desire to be with friends, at times circumstances prevent it. Steadfast and faithful friends understand the demands in life that sometimes get in the way. Equally important, learn to accept the demands and limitations your friends experience too. Mutual understanding and presuming the best in each other strengthens ties. Ultimately, shared grace between friends will make your time together in the future more satisfying.

What you can do:

• You'll probably never be able to have enough time or interest for everyone. Remember, you can't *do* everything or *be* everything for everyone. Accept your limits and remind yourself frequently that it's okay to spend time with friends who matter most.

• Before you respond to a request or invitation from someone, learn to say: "Let me think about it." Consider every new commitment carefully and make sure each decision you make about your time will be the right one for you.

Part of good self-care is learning when to say yes and when to say no. Bona fide friends understand both without the need for justification.

• Set personal priorities for yourself, even if it means some people won't be happy with you. Don't waste valuable time frozen in guilt, or in need of reassurance from others.

Both are useless emotions and prevent you from acting on important needs.

• Different friends meet different needs. Accept the fact that you might not be the chosen person at the top of your friend's "to call" list. Always presume the best and give them the benefit of the doubt.

Learn To Refuel

For women, unquestionably, time for self is often the first to go. Balancing time for yourself is essential to good mental, physical, and spiritual health. It's hard to give to others when you haven't had time to give to yourself. To be your best in friendships, don't forget to value your needs and practice good self-care whenever you can.

Tita has shared the proactive attitude and behaviors she holds when it comes to making friends a priority and managing her time. But she also recognizes her need for alone time, which also is a priority. She has learned it gives her the energy to be in the relationships she loves. She says:

> I have limits. Believe me, I do. It doesn't happen often, but once in awhile four or five friends will converge on me all at once wanting to schedule time together all in the same week. I can't do it. I won't let other relationships with my kids and husband suffer, and I won't let my relationship with me suffer either. Again, you have to stay in balance and figure out what that balance is for you. I've learned for me, spending time with two friends a week is perfect. If someone is in crisis, that's different. I'm going to be there for them no matter what. But if I become too drained, I know I have to be alone. I like alone time, and I use it to refuel. I want to have plenty of fuel for all my relationships, and the way to do it is to re-

treat, have solitude, and take care of me. That's how I can make time for friends; by tuning in to my need for alone time and making sure I get it. My closest friends know and honor that.

What you can do:

- Make the choice to slow down and refuel in order to avoid burnout.
- Treat yourself to alone time and boost your energy. Schedule it in. Read, walk, decorate, shop, write, pray, paint, garden, bake, sew, build something, run, exercise, swim … or just take a nap.
- Support your friends when they have time to be with you and when they don't. Remember everyone needs alone time, and taking time to be revitalized benefits you both the next time you spend together.
- Role model good self-care for one another.

When To Seek Further Help

If you have difficulty coping with a hurried life that causes you daily distress, seek out additional support. If one or more of the following issues apply to you, consider obtaining professional assistance.

Behavior checklist:

- Anxiety
- Continual sense of urgency
- Depression
- Distractibility
- Fear of failure
- Over-accessibility
- Over-scheduling
- Overwhelming stress
- Perfectionism

- Procrastination
- Worry

You can improve and often completely overcome difficulties that seem to define or overshadow parts of your personality. Habitual ways of reacting to life often serve a purpose. Positive or negative, behaviors start for a reason. Perhaps chronic over-scheduling helps you circumvent feelings of emptiness or escape an unhappy marriage. Most people can learn to recognize the meanings behind certain behaviors and gain the insight necessary to improve them. Great relief can come from confronting and modifying behaviors that prevent you from feeling a sense of satisfaction and peace in how you're living each day.

Soul Solutions

You were created by God to need the friendship of women and to be needed by them too. Friendship then is designed to bless you and them at the same time. It's a mutual commitment, and in both receiving and giving, the beauty of friendship is formed. Spending time with women friends is a priority that, when met, does not disappoint.

As the old hymn goes, "Blessed be the ties that bind, our hearts in Christian love...." Ties that stay connected create bonds that are rarely torn apart. This is stated beautifully in Ecclesiastes 4:10,12 (NIV). Ties that bind require time to grow and form. They also need tending and strengthening on a regular basis.

In the busyness of your life, you may be feeling a variety of emotions after reading this chapter. Before moving on to the next, allow God to help you begin sorting through your needs and priorities. Your desires may be many, so you may want to jot down a few of them in the margin while they're fresh in your mind. Reflect on the areas with which you want help and direction or simply choose this time to sit quietly.

Prayer Guide

Close your eyes for a few minutes and relax. Seek God and His faithful presence to help you wash away any frustration or uncertainty. What are the needs and priorities of which you are currently most aware? When these are clear and you feel peace and confirmation, close your eyes in gratitude as you come before Him.

Some of you may feel completely beleaguered knowing how many changes are needed in trying to learn to appreciate "this very moment" and the friends in your life. Others of you may feel confirmed knowing that you are spending your time enjoying activities and seeing friends that you value. Either way, you are not alone. Spending time in prayer can console you and help you seek the right solutions for your life. Prayer may also affirm your current path.

What you can do:

• When you commit to the act of prayer, you are practicing the greatest form of mindfulness. This intimate communication between you and God can help reduce blood pressure and stress. Carve out spiritual quiet time with God for yourself each day. Stop, be still, and pray. Seek the answers to your questions and ask for what you need or desire. Learn to patiently listen for God's will in all situations.

• If finding quiet time to pray is difficult for you, consider listening to CDs to uplift you in the car or at home.

• Pursue quiet and solitude with God in nature. Daily time spent outdoors in God's presence can bring balance and direction to a busy life. "Cease striving and know that I am God..." Psalm 46:10.

Spending time with God in prayer and in His Word will enlighten you much more than any words written on this page. May you find His goodness plentiful in your friendships today.

Closing Scripture

Consider these verses and how you can put them into action and attitude. Take note of how these critical qualities make a difference in your relationships.

> *Now as they were traveling along, He entered a village; and a woman named Martha welcomed Him into her home. She had a sister called Mary, who was seated at the Lord's feet, listening to His word. But Martha was distracted with all her preparations; and she came up to Him and said, "Lord, do You not care that my sister has left me to do all the serving alone? Then tell her to help me." But the Lord answered and said to her, "Martha, Martha, you are worried and bothered about so many things; but only one thing is necessary, for Mary has chosen the good part, which shall not be taken away from her"* (Luke 10:38-42).

Friend-to-Friend Activities

1. Highs & Lows

Share the high point and the low point of your day with a friend. Both high and low points in life can be important experiences to learn from. The simple act of identifying the positive and negative events of a day and expressing them to someone supportive can relieve stress. Open up and share a mutual exchange of honest thoughts and feelings, and offer encouragement to one another.

2. VIF (Very Important Friend) List

Name five friends that help you through thick and thin. When was the last time you spent time with each one? Next, make a list of the needs you are aware of today. For example, do you need laughter, accountability, recreation, adventure, or just a good listener? Which friend might help meet this need? Put that person's name and number on your to-do list and schedule time to spend with her.

3. Stress Scale

Sit down with a friend, and together draw a scale from one to five. One on the scale represents no stress, and five represents the most stress you've ever experienced. First, rate your own level of stress and then evaluate your perceptions of your friend's current time demands and stress loads. Take turns discussing your own rating and then the number you chose for your friend. What changes do you notice? What concerns do you have for one another? Remember to point out the positive changes and behaviors you see too. Brainstorm how you can support each other in either bringing your numbers down or maintaining low levels of stress.

Chapter 2

Obstacles

> We've been friends a long time, despite the fact our religious beliefs are on opposite ends of the spectrum. You find solace through your belief in God . . . I wish I could believe also, but as you know, I fit somewhere in-between an agnostic and atheist. —*Elke (age 60)*

Women are a mixed bag of values, beliefs, and lifestyles. Differences between people can make life interesting, thought-provoking, and fun, or create major roadblocks in personal relationships. For most women, finding compatibility and acceptance between friends who don't think, believe, or live life in quite the same way is challenging.

Obstacles can block, delay, interrupt, or simply create an inconvenience in friendships. Common barriers might include: conflicting political views, diverse religious beliefs, geographical distance, personality traits, life transitions, or lifestyles. Sometimes they feel like insurmountable hurdles. The frustration may prevent women from being able to enjoy and draw closer to friends—or put a halt to friendships altogether.

An ideal scenario is when friends who genuinely love one another can flex and bend around their philosophical and lifestyle differences. But women acknowledge that it's not easy to do this, even when they wish they could. Obviously, there are many things that pave the road to long-lasting friendships. An important component to their long-term survival is how obstacles are approached and handled. For any friendship, changing your attitude about a problem can help diffuse negative feelings and responses.

Obstacles Can Be Opportunities

Obstacles may interrupt and test a friendship, but they can also provide opportunities. In fact, even seemingly insurmountable barriers can be the catalyst for personal growth. Jamie (age 50) said:

> It's important to welcome friends with differences into my life—even the big ones, like ideas or choices I think I could never handle or accept in anyone. It broadens my point of view and it's good. Contrary to what some might think, my faith is strengthened by differing views and beliefs. Healthy debate and exploration keeps me growing. It's easy to love people who are like me. It's not so easy when they aren't. That's what makes it so rewarding.

When you have friends who hold conflicting views or are experiencing transitions in life, ask yourself: What needs to happen to make this friendship work? How can we stay connected? What extra effort can we make to remain friends? When a friendship is important enough, most obstacles provide the opportunity to broaden each person's perspective and help each one grow in interesting and unexpected ways. Dee (age 52) believes friends contribute to her understanding of the world, especially when they are very different from her. She says:

> My friends are like crowbars. They pry me open and expand my point of view. They prevent me from becoming rigid and closed in my thinking. The world is big, the culture is complex, and intelligent Christian women have a responsibility to understand those outside their safe circle of ideas and beliefs.

Solutions

Overcoming obstacles in friendships can be approached like any other deterrent in life. For example, if you walk several times a week to improve your physical and mental health, or for the mere pleasure of it, does the rain have to stop you? Probably not. Instead, you put on rain gear and head outside. When you face gridlock in traffic because of an accident, or construction work, what do you do? Go home? That's doubtful. Instead, you wait, assess the situation and continue on, or look for a detour and go around it. On a hike up a steep mountain, you might feel powerless to scale its impossible looking height. Do you immediately give up? Usually you won't. If you're determined to reach the top you'll stop, rest, and refuel when necessary to reach your intended goal. Each scenario takes personal effort and a sincere desire to accomplish, but a person makes the effort because the activity holds value for them. The benefits are immediate and measurable. Making something important happen is worth the inconvenience.

You can conquer just about any obstacle as long as you are committed to it. If your attitude is positive and your thinking is constructive, you can trigger a series of assorted, workable outcomes in any friendship situation. Practice integrating the proactive ways of thinking listed below. They will not only positively affect your attitude and effort, but by putting them into action, they affirm your friends. Keep these in mind as you work through each of the specific obstacles that follow in this chapter, as well as any other hurdles unique to your friendships:

• *Acceptance says:* "Please explain how you feel. I want to understand why we think differently about this. I can accept this change in our friendship because you matter so much to me."

• *Respect confirms:* "I accept and am tolerant of what is true for you. I admire your ability to do what's best for you. I value who you are and why you feel the way you do."

• *Perseverance asserts:* "We'll get through this change. We can hang in there until it smoothes itself out or we find our way through it. We may fall down, but we can help each other up. We'll adjust to each other accordingly."

• *Patience affirms:* "I'm not going to worry—I know in time we'll be okay. Let's give this phase of our friendship time to settle. We've got staying power."

• *Joy exclaims:* "What an amazing adventure! I wouldn't have experienced this if it hadn't been for you. I am grateful we are open to becoming better friends despite our differences. I am a happier person for having you in my life."

• *Humor reminds:* "Let's laugh and play. There's always a good story to tell and a humorous way to look at this. It will become even more hilarious with time. Though we are opposites when it comes to this issue, our different take on it can't change the humor and laughter we share!"

• *Love shows:* "I appreciate who you are, and I care about you. You have changed and expanded my life. I want you as my friend."

Politics and Religion

Hindrances to solid friendships are varied and many, but two stand out above all others: politics and religion.

Unquestionably, differing religious and political values can create enormous barriers that aren't always overcome—world history proves it. Nevertheless, in friendships even the most sensitive subjects can shift from being an obstacle to an opportunity when approached with a reasonable, open, and caring attitude.

There are a number of moral issues and political positions that can separate friends. Theological debates, separation of church and state, sexual orientation, abortion, gun control, prayer in schools, and the death penalty are just a few of the many controversial topics frequently making headlines. Conservative, moderate, liberal, or undecided—your political stance may set you apart from one friend or even groups of friends. When friendships are strained, uncomfortable, or at-risk because you can't see eye-to-eye on an issue, your differences can feel awkward, and any arguments can become unusually heated.

Naturally, women's feelings on these hot-button issues are all over the board. Rosetta (age 58) says this: "I try not to dwell on differences about religion and politics. What matters to me is my friendships, so it works best for me to stay off the controversial topics."

Yet, Bonnie (age 58) feels differently:

> For me, it's important that my close friends share my faith. I not only want that for them, but our common belief in God creates a bond that is greater than other common interests. I realize that the kind of deep friendship I seek comes mostly through friends who believe like me.

As Elke stated in the opening of this chapter, her beliefs fall somewhere between an agnostic and atheist. As a non-Christian, Elke, shares more from her perspective:

I only have one friend who believes that we will not go to heaven if we do not accept Christ into our lives. That part is most perplexing to me about Christian faith. I hope that God would take into account good people, living good lives, and the good things each one has contributed to this world.

Linda (age 45) said:

I think women have more of a problem with this than men. When women don't agree about something deeply important to them, most think they can't have a friendship ... as if they can't disagree and still be friends. Men get right past it and just accept each other; I'm more like a man that way. I'm a liberal, but some of my best friends are very conservative. And it's fine. We don't agree—big deal! There's always more to people than where they stand on war and the death penalty.

Others don't agree. One woman said

If I have to debate a controversial issue with someone, we probably won't end up being close friends. Scripture is clear on all the moral issues. There should be no question about what is right or wrong. It's a given in my close friendships.

Patty (age 54) said:

I think it's great when I form a strong bond with a friend who is my exact opposite in every way! As Christians, we're taught to accept and not to judge. So whatever political end someone's on, and whatever their faith, religion, or lack thereof; I think their

> position requires my utmost respect. Giving respect doesn't diminish my Christian belief; it just makes me faithful to it.

Religious and political perspectives are part of the foundation on which people build their lives. Deep convictions resonate from the heart and soul. They can't be dismissed, nor should they. What is paramount for one is unimportant to the other. These women represent friends everywhere who, day in and day out, are spending time together in each other's homes, the workplace, and restaurants. They are all across America—and the world. One of the above perspectives, or something close to it, is likely yours.

What makes women able to stand firm with a friend, rather than avoid or flee, when substantial religious or political obstacles enter their relationship? Chandler (age 57) answers:

> I have a couple of friends who have pretty different spiritual views from mine. Fortunately, it has never been a true obstacle for us. We've made a deliberate choice to respect each other's beliefs, and we talk about it openly. Our discussions are true sharing of hearts and minds. In talking about our differences, we've been better able to understand the reasons behind the positions we've taken, and that alone helps us better understand and accept our unique viewpoints.

Friends like these have put their love, acceptance, and respect for one another into action. These deeds are admirable because they are not always easy to do. At times Christians may feel they must correct, challenge, or defend positions in opposition to their own in order to help someone. You may need to use restraint and self-control, but when you're confident in your own religious beliefs, differing ones do not have to feel threatening. Feeling obliged to point out what you believe to be faulty thoughts or feelings is an unwelcome intrusion for most. Imposing your beliefs on someone rarely results in the outcome you might desire. In fact, usually it has the opposite effect, and you end up pushing people further away. Remember, God does not need to be defended. He's big enough to take care of Himself.

Although Christianity does call believers to proclaim its message and be a witness to others, how it's done speaks louder than words. First Peter 3:15 (NIV) gives one example of what Christians are called to do: "Always be prepared to give an answer to everyone who asks you to give the reason for the hope that you have. But do this with gentleness and respect." Peter's last word in the verse is *respect*. When respect is present, opportunities are plentiful to talk and explore further. This can be true of any personal belief or stance. Mutual consideration is the key that keeps friendships from being torn apart and left in a heap of hurt feelings.

Elke and her Christian friend both recognize beliefs are based on very personal decisions. In a climate of mutual respect, they've discovered it's possible to feel free to give and take, without anxiety, and share their deepest thoughts without compromising their own beliefs. Elke understands why differing religious beliefs aren't a negative in her close friendship with a Christian woman. Her sincerity of heart is clear as she explains in a unique, German accent:

> I have always enjoyed observing how much comfort my Christian friend draws from her faith, and I could not imagine why she would not feel compelled to share her belief of salvation with all the people she

> cares about. So, in a way I have felt loved when she tells me she wants me to be saved. She has always shown me respect and tact. I have never been made to feel uncomfortable by her need to share with me the promise of eternal life that she believes in.

Elke's Christian friend said this about her:

> She asks questions, and I'm able to open up and ask her questions right back. I've grown in many ways from the things she's shared. I'm not sure she even begins to realize how unusual this is. Elke has always cared that I wanted to share my faith with her, and never once has she been indifferent to it. It's huge to me. In return I've tried to always show respect for her beliefs. I've told her a million times, but I just keep saying it again; her accepting and respectful attitude means so much to me.

Despite their differing philosophies, Elke and her friend prove that friendship can flourish even when pivotal differences exist. Like so many women, raising children together, they shared creative and leisure interests and an abundance of humor and laughter that reinforced their relationship. Most of all, Elke and her friend's love for one another has prevailed.

Women benefit in innumerable ways by sharing ideas, beliefs, and opinions with one another. That's why so many women say they love to spend time together. Relationships can become more intimate and authentic through frank discussion.

What you can do:

- Remain open-minded; consciously respect your friend's differences.

• Be curious rather than judgmental. Listen, ask, and observe. Make the deliberate choice to be interested rather than critical of positions different from your own.

• There is much more to friendship than personal worldviews that create deadlock. What common history do you share that overrides such obstacles?

• If it's important to both of you, take the time to share your ideas, beliefs, and feelings together with the goal of growing an intimate, more understanding and appreciative friendship.

• Hold your friends' opinions in high regard, even when you strongly disagree. Respect is the cornerstone of friendship. Different points of view paint a more interesting picture, and they guarantee lively discussions and stimulating time together.

• Which qualities of acceptance, respect, perseverance, patience, joy, humor, or love can you put into action to help you overcome the obstacles you experience with friends? To motivate you to take action on one of the above qualities, ask yourself, "Why do I want this friend in my life? What are the qualities that I love about her?"

Across the Miles: Geographical Distance

> I always end up living in different cities than my closest friends. I have grown so weary of saying goodbye… —*Michelle (age 32)*

As the saying goes, "Absence makes the heart grow fonder," but geographical distance only represents another frustrating challenge for many women who are close friends. For some it's too much of an obstacle. Trish (35) said, "Being separated makes my heart grow sadder, not fonder. It's not the same living so far apart now. I couldn't stay connected, and I hate admitting it, but I have let the friendship go."

It's not uncommon for friends to grow apart over time and distance. Expecting closeness to continue across the miles isn't always realistic, but it's definitely possible. Even though long spans of time without contact can challenge a friendship, a number of women attested to the fact that it is possible to maintain close relationships even when they are separated by thousands of miles. Laurie (age 41) said surprises and regular communication are two ways to make it work:

> Even though our lives have literally gone in different directions, the bond we created has kept us close. Rare is the week that I don't get a message on my answering machine, "just checking in," or a letter in the mail with the latest baby or vacation photos. Frequently I get e-mail messages with a joke for the day or words of comfort about something going on in my life. My friends have shown up for surprise birthday parties, sent flowers for no reason, and one of them even drove five hours just to watch my daughter's first piano recital.

Staying connected and involved despite a geographical distance requires greater commitment and planning. It's not always fifty-fifty, give and take; sometimes it's ninety-ten. But women say with mutual effort and perseverance, a move to a distant city or state does not have to signal the end of an important friendship.

Many women say distance requires an extraordinary bond. Melinda (age 43) describes hers:

> Ironically, my closest friend is the one furthest

> away—958 miles north to be exact. She moved fifteen years ago after knowing me for only two years. The fact that she is still my closest friend speaks to the powerful and immediate connection we both felt when we first met. I still believe God made this bond the way it is because we were destined to live apart for the rest of our lives. He knew our friendship would have to be strong. And it is. We have phone dates now every other Saturday, and we plan trips to meet each other in different cities once a year. Our time together is like Christmas morning. I can hardly wait for it to get here, and then it's over way too soon.

Maintaining long distance friendships is not only possible, but it can be exciting too. Just because you're far away doesn't mean you have to lose closeness, humor, or time together. Demi and her friend, both in their early 50s, have stayed connected despite the miles between them. Demi describes the bond that keeps their friendship intact and growing:

> I met my best friend in the fifth grade. We spent one year together before she moved to another city. Forty years later, guess what? We not only remain the best of friends, but when we are together, it's as if we've never been apart. At age twelve, we wrote each other twenty page letters; at sixteen, we took train trips; in our twenties, we flew to each other's weddings; and since then we started calling and emailing regularly. We have "in person" visits every chance we get. Our sense of humor is still back in the fifth grade (but we like to think, even then, we were more clever than most). Our daughters think it's amazing.

> We pray for the same experience for them someday. And our husbands are friends now too, so our time together just grows more interesting all the time. Our friendship gives us great security in life. It's a reminder of how good life can be . . . even with hundreds of miles between us. Time and distance do not matter a bit. We pick up right where we left off.

A fresh perspective can also be valuable. A 39-year-old woman illustrates how attitude can change your point of view when distance is involved: "Up front, you just accept the fact that your long distance friendship will be different. No better, no worse—just different. What's the alternative? For me, it's far easier to accept it's going to be different than to accept that it has to end."

"Thelma and Louise," now in their late 40s, are long distance friends too. Like a lot of women, they adopted the movie duo names for fun. They especially like using this alias when they feel rebellious or stressed out. It provides comic relief and instant camaraderie despite living at opposite ends of the country. Thelma explains it like this:

> I really miss Louise. I have free weekend minutes on my cell so we talk for hours at a time nearly every week. But here's the interesting thing: I'm a Christian; she's a Buddhist. I live on the west coast; she lives on the east coast. She loves cats; I love dogs. I'm married; she's not. She's not a mother; I am. I wear makeup, and she doesn't. I hate crafts, and she loves them. She goes for opera; I prefer rock. She reads Shakespeare, and well, I just read other things. It goes on and on. You'd think we might not get along. But the fact is we do. We not only get along, but we laugh until we cry and can't breathe.

> We laugh about finding a fast car and a steep cliff, but the truth is our sense of humor bonds us and makes life good. We spill our guts to each other, and it never matters how things come out or how much sense it really makes. We sort through the good and the bad and never stop laughing. It's been that way since we were two years old, always there for each other through thick and thin. I picked up the phone last night and heard, "Thelma?" I knew something was wrong. "How bad is it?" I asked. "Fire up the engine; we're gonna take a drive!" I told her I'd get the keys. We laughed and made the world right again. She's a steady and constant friend in my life, whether she's next door or 3,000 miles away.

Women like Thelma and Louise love and appreciate the best in each other. One can be strong when the other is weak; they warn each other of unwise decisions, revel together in successes, and give a boost to one another in failures. This kind of love, support, and encouragement can travel any distance. You can adopt the mindset that distance won't diminish friendship; the miles between you simply allow your friendship to take new forms.

The women who shared in this section are walking proof that strong links are rarely broken when mutual commitment thrives. Let them be mentors of encouragement for the long-distance friends you are thinking of or missing today.

What you can do:

- Make a commitment to preserve and nurture the friendships you value. Say it out loud to each other, then agree on a realistic way to do this. There are many possibilities, and you'll gain momentum with a positive attitude.

• Change distance into opportunity. See your time together as a chance to do something out of the ordinary, new, and exciting.

• Be creative. Untie the strings; think outside the box. For example, two women said they meet once a year at a conference. They arrive early and stay late to make the most of their time together.

• Start your own tradition or "friendition," that you can look forward to every year. It might be a new place to hike every autumn, enjoy a "high tea" in the summer, or spend a weekend at the beach for birthdays. Even a relaxing spa treatment every spring could become an annual event. Meeting at annual quilt fairs, rodeos, plays, or concerts are other ideas women shared. Take turns planning the activity within your group of long-distance friends, and over time you will have fun taking part in a variety of locations, interests and travel experiences.

• Infuse humor into your relationship whenever you can. Call a friend just to have a good laugh. You need no other excuse than just to tell her something funny. Laughter is beneficial any time, packs an incredible punch, and helps preserve long-distance connections—it's a tie that binds.

• Pick up the phone—Set dates and times; take turns calling.

• E-mail, e-mail, e-mail. Show you care. Always respond—even if it's only a few words.

• Send snail mail—cards, jokes, poems, notes, newspaper clippings, pictures, small gifts, big gifts—a monthly box of chocolate—whatever is meaningful between the two of you.

• Meet halfway—enjoy a completely new city, a shared activity, or a vacation or special event. Plan to do it annually. At the end of your trip, set a date for the next one.

• Which qualities of acceptance, respect, perseverance,

patience, joy, humor, or love can you put into action to help you overcome the challenge of living a long distance from a friend? To motivate you to take action on one of the above qualities, ask yourself, "Why do I want this friend in my life? What qualities do I love about her?" and "How important is it to stay connected?"

Personality Traits

It comes as no surprise that life brings friends with a blend of temperaments and personalities. Life would be boring without all the variations that exist between people. Visualize for a minute your friends as an assortment of fabrics, each one woven with different colors and textures. Some are sewn to form bold, cheerful geometric blends, while others resemble practical, orderly cottons. Some are strong, forceful corduroys, and still others are sensitive, peaceful blends of satin or lace. Who you choose for a friend, and who you "click" with are often dependent on the personality traits you are drawn to and with which you feel most comfortable.

While no one fits a single personality description perfectly, most people are born with a particular temperament that stays with them throughout life. By nature, shy women may be more introverted their entire life. However, depending on the environment women grow up in, adult role models, and all aspects of the socialization process, they may overcome the negative or painful aspects sometimes accompanied by shyness. Likewise, if by nature women tend to be extroverted and impulsive, they may learn over time how to be better listeners, become more cautious and organized, and think things through before taking action.

Most people are made up of a combination of different traits, and it's through these varying combinations that friends may clash, overstep, and misunderstand one another. A talkative, outgoing, or loud woman may not always enjoy being with a friend who is quiet, calm, and prefers to sit back and observe rather than participate. In a case like this, it's easy to feel judgmental and frustrated. Personality differences are often not recognized as the cause for difficulties, and time and again become unspoken obstacles that hinder meaningful friendships.

Marj (age 40) says,

> It's hard for me to be with a friend of mine even though I really like her! She is always so "out there," always noticed and popular with everyone. It makes me feel invisible when I say something and no one seems to even hear me. I come away feeling bad about myself, thinking I'm boring even though I know I'm not. It doesn't happen with anyone else but her.

Personality differences may cause you to perceive, relate, and interact with the world in very different ways. It's easy to think one trait is stronger or better than another; but the truth is, there's no right or wrong, good or bad, worse or better personality trait. Differences only confirm how people are special and unique. Accepting a friend's traits unconditionally is not always easy, but imagine how dull and lacking the world would be without this diversity.

What you can do:

- Recognize every friend serves a unique purpose within your life.
- Talk to your friend about the different ways the two of you relate to the world and other people. If you feel ignored because of your friend's outgoing personality, ask her to help

you feel more included. Extroverts are usually great at being inclusive, and often have skills to bring people together. On the other end of the spectrum, if you're an outgoing person, you may need to ask your introverted friends to help you slow down, relax, and concentrate on what you came together to do.

• Make every effort to understand and bear the weaknesses of one another. Every person has a combination of strengths and weaknesses. Choose to focus on strengths. A willingness to overlook weaknesses often means the difference between a short-term and long-term friendship.

• Remember to be appreciative and humble for what is both perfect and imperfect in your friend and within yourself. You are both unique, yet both flawed.

• Adopt a viewpoint of love and acceptance, respecting those in your life who may be quite opposite in personality. If you are polar opposites, enjoy how your strengths can positively influence one another. See life from each other's viewpoint. It can help both of you develop new awareness and insight. In the words of George Santayana: "In each person I catch the fleeting suggestion of something beautiful and swear eternal friendship with that."

• Think about your closest friends. Do their strengths bring opportunities and benefits to you? Do you see weaknesses that create obstacles for you? Can you talk with them about it, from a position of respect and love?

• Which qualities of acceptance, respect, perseverance, patience, joy, humor, or love can you put into action to help you overcome negative attitudes towards certain traits in friends? To motivate you to take action on one of the above qualities, ask yourself: Why do I want this friend in my life? What qualities do I love about her?

Transition and Change

Heraclitus said, "Everything flows, nothing stays still." Everything in life is constantly moving and changing. Very little stays the same. People and circumstances shift and realign too. That's life, and it's good to move forward. There's no stopping the seasons as they come and go, and there's no stopping the change and transition that inevitably touch friendships.

As change occurs in relationships, friends must adjust, or as someone once said, "Accept change and grow, or resist and remain." Repeatedly women confirm this. A 55-year-old woman said: "Transition and change is a fact of life. Friends move into my life, and friends move out of my life. If I can't bridge a gap that is getting wider because interests, life, and priorities change, I generally accept it's time to move on."

In spite of numerous changes, many women remain constant, lifelong friends. Others, however, don't survive the transitions they must weather. There isn't enough time or space to hold on to everyone you enjoy, even when that's your desire.

Kris (age 44) echoes the opinion of many:

> Why do friends only last as long as we live in a neighborhood? We've moved three times in the same city, and I'm tired of not keeping my old neighborhood friends. I guess I could do more to stay in touch, so why don't I?

Many of life's circumstances create obstacles that can be hard to maneuver around. Illness, physical disabilities, divorce, marriage, children, empty nest, career change, financial freedom or hardships, and even moving a few blocks away are examples of what can impact friendships at one time or another.

Margaret (age 47) regrets some of the changes she sees happening with friends:

> Even though we aren't that old, physical incompatibility is a challenge that is coming up more frequently among my friends. Sometimes I want to spend time together on a hike or a bike ride like we used to, and they aren't able to do it. This happens more than you think, and does limit certain friendships."

Terri (age 52) says attitudes change to:

> Fear. Is it just my imagination, or are a lot of my friends getting more fearful as they get older? It's frustrating to me, because just when we have a little more money and freedom, I see some of my friends getting poorer, in the sense that they are getting narrow in their scope of how they see their lives. I want to expand and have more adventure in my life! They want to stay home in their comfortable routines.

Both of these are examples of circumstances where women can offer compassion and support, and maybe a little inspiration. Sometimes changing old habits and a willingness to make concessions and sacrifices are required. If it can't work, women may choose to move on or find alternative ways to be in the friendship.

Tracey (age 49) reveals an alternative that works for her:

> My friend, Lori, is chronically ill. Her friendship is an enriching experience for me, and I believe for her too. It's limited in ways and forces me to nurture and listen more, but it's the role I accepted, so our friendship can still flourish. What I've learned in the

> past year is that what she needs from me more than anything is some distraction, fun, and humor. I've allowed myself to be more lighthearted, and it's come out in her too. We laugh and joke more than we did the first twelve years of our friendship, even in the midst of her chronic pain. I feel good knowing this has helped her get outside her problems sometimes. This has strengthened our friendship in an unexpected way.

Common bonds unite women, keeping them connected, vibrant, and strong even through transition and change. At other times, women find themselves simply going through the motions in a friendship that has faded because of too many personal and life changes. Pretense and obligation never work for long. A genuine and sincere desire for connection is essential for relationships you value; otherwise it may be best to keep it casual and relate as friendly, but passing acquaintances. Inevitably, pretending will force any friendship to unravel in hurtful, unhealthy ways.

Transitions come in many forms. Sometimes change must signal the end of a friendship with one person, and a new chapter begins with others. Connie (age 50) says.

> I have to say that I am in a strange place in my life. I find that I need only one or two close friends anymore and that's all. I speak around the country, spend time with a lot of women and thoroughly enjoy it, but then I look forward to coming back to my study and writing. As someone who is generally outgoing and very social, this is a huge change for me. Many friends don't get it, and sometimes I feel I have less and less in common with them.

Whether transition is chosen due to a career change or

forced, unplanned circumstances, choices have to be made. It's not always easy for those who are not the ones changing.

A 35-year-old woman said: "I want my old friend back. It's not the same anymore." She's right. People and places don't stay the same. Friendships are a challenge to save sometimes; they must be renewed, grow, and adapt to changes; otherwise they will wither away. Finding a new normal with friends in the midst of changed personalities and situations is difficult, and frankly, isn't always possible.

Alison (age 51) illustrates with this example:

> I have two friends I'm growing further and further apart from. Our history is all we have left in common. They are both newly divorced, and mid-life divorces are particularly messy, since they often accompany bizarre behavior by one of the partners with affairs and dramatic, unexpected changes. Anyway, it feels uncomfortable and too different to stay involved in.

Letting go of people is necessary sometimes. It's the only way for friends to move on and address different needs and priorities that must take precedence at particular junctures in life. Nothing takes away the value or influence each person has added to your life. Remaining appreciative for a friend as you both go separate ways is a bitter-sweet experience, but it's a reality sometimes.

What you can do:

- Accept change and learn to welcome it, rather than to fear it, or to feel threatened by it in others. When seen as an opportunity, change can be the catalyst for growth. Remember that all relationships move through stages and transitions. Try to compromise, or inspire your friend to stretch and grow with you. Survive those you can, and move on from those you can't.

• When you can, accept the limitations that might be forced on important friendships. Your commitment to a friend is only as strong as the value you hold for her. When a friend is highly valued, concessions can be made with little, if any, effect on the relationship.

• Loyal friends can live through "thick and thin." Loyalty comes naturally and is not forced. Be authentic and real.

• Which qualities of acceptance, respect, perseverance, patience, joy, humor, or love can you put into action to help you overcome the fear of change or adjustment to transitions in life? To motivate you to take action on one of the above qualities, ask yourself: Why do I want this friend in my life? What qualities do I love about her?

Lifestyle Differences

Outside observers may not understand how Thelma and Louise, illustrated earlier in this chapter, could ever become friends. They admit they are as different as night and day and in some areas almost complete opposites. Sometimes outsiders are quick to judge and even criticize friendship choices women make. People are creatures of habit and comfortable seeing people who appear to "go together." When lifestyles are very different, it may be hard to see how relationships can form, let alone last. But they can, and they do—every day.

Your marital status, income, education, parenting, and career choices all represent lifestyle differences that can impede or even prevent a friendship. All require you to adjust, bend, and flex. The old exercise motto, "no pain, no gain" may be true when your friend's way of life differs from your own. However, some lifestyle differences present obstacles that may be too big to handle. Here is what Tracey (age 49) shared:

> I am single, but my friend Rhonda is married with seven children. She isn't free to get away, and when we try to get together, her children dominate our time together. Because all her time is consumed with her kids, it is always difficult to engage in adult conversation. It is the way it is with kids—constant interruptions. The only way I could continue my friendship with Rhonda was to accept the limitations always having children around would bring. Since I have more freedom and flexibility, the great majority of the compromise pretty much had to be with me. I had to give up my needs. After fifteen years of this, it wasn't very enjoyable or satisfying to me. I had a lot of guilt about disconnecting from our friendship because I understood it was not her fault that she was busy with her kids, but I feel you have to be able to connect on something. Whatever it is, you have to be able to share thoughts and feelings, and enjoy one another—and be able to do something together. You can make all the allowances you want for your differences, but at some point, sooner or later, if you're not able to enjoy some things that appeal to both, it's difficult to connect in ways that are mutually satisfying. We finally parted ways because we couldn't find anything to talk about anymore.

It's necessary for women to find some common ground in their lives in order to relate to one another. It can be absolutely anything from chocolate to a master's thesis. Lesli (age 39) chuckled and said: "I have one friend who sees the humor in life just the same way I do. We get silly every time we're around each other, and all we do is laugh! No one else seems to 'get it' but us, which makes us laugh even harder. We're connected at the funny bone!"

Whatever it is, the connection has to happen to give you reason to want to get together. Then it needs to be sustained. Oftentimes bonds are evident the minute you meet, but at other times, you are pleasantly surprised to find a kindred spirit as you get to know each other. Either way, there needs to be something that ties your interests, activities, or passions—a certain something that draws your hearts and minds together.

Angie (age 36), a stay-at-home mom, tells us how motherhood impacted friendships for her. With so many mothers working today, her experience is a common one.

> During that isolated time of young motherhood when I first became a stay-at-home mom, I became desperately lonely. All of my friends and neighbors worked, and I found our interests and schedules drifting apart. I didn't have anyone like me to spend time with, and I missed having support and friendship to look forward to.

Stay-at-home moms, especially ones new to the role, may be especially vulnerable to loneliness and isolation. They may feel guilty for spending time away from little ones to be with friends, or lack the opportunities to form friendships. It's a challenge for them, but an opportunity for others who feel called to mentor new mothers.

Beth (age 42) raises this question:

> I have a completely different lifestyle dilemma. Why do many women who have children assume if you don't have children, your life is not satisfying and

> full? I find this very frustrating since I do enjoy my life, even though it does not include being a mother."

Women without children, whether by choice or happenstance, can be offended by this bias or assumption. All women, whether with or without children, have doors of purpose, passion and enjoyment that God opens to them. Women who are mothers need to remember this about women who aren't.

Connie (age 57) experiences a different lifestyle challenge: women who find themselves single again after many years of marriage. She explains:

> After my divorce I found myself missing not being included in family activities with my married friends. If I had a significant other, I think my social life would improve dramatically because "we" would be included in more social events. I miss the dinners out, camping trips, and family barbecues my daughters and I used to enjoy so much before the divorce.

Some social situations and lifestyle differences cannot be remedied, but many can be successfully overcome. Consider the following suggestions to help solve or improve the challenges you face.

What you can do:

- Consider whether or not the obstacle you are facing is worthy of discussion. Ask yourself: Can you move forward comfortably with your friend without conversation on this topic? If so, accept this difference in lifestyle and enjoy the aspects of the friendship that work for you.
- Avoidance does not bring unity and peace. If a friendship is important to you, and the obstacle significant, do not

avoid discussing the issue. Always consider being the one to take the initiative to speak in loving frankness if an issue stands between you. For more guidance in this area, you can refer to the "Art of Confrontation" in Chapter three.

• Be sure it is the obstacle, and not the person, you wish to change.

• Loving another person means it's important to be willing at times to change yourself.

• Community centers and churches often have organizations, groups, and activities that give stay-at-home mothers many opportunities to connect with one another. Few things require more commitment and responsibility than that of a mother, so if you find yourself feeling alone, seek out new friends who share your present lifestyle.

• Find substitutes for family activities you miss if you are divorced or single. For example, volunteer to accompany a class on an outing, or chaperone on longer trips involving travel. Fundraising activities, clubs, and sports teams are other ways to join and meet others of both sexes! Rather than wait to be invited to a family social event, plan your own. Invite families and friends to your house; show them how you enjoy spending time with them, and how you want to stay involved socially.

Which qualities of acceptance, respect, perseverance, patience, joy, humor, or love can you put into action to help you overcome the challenge of different lifestyles? To motivate you to take action on one of the above qualities, ask yourself: Why do I want this friend in my life? What qualities do I love about her?

There are times when obstacles are truly insurmountable. If parting ways is an inevitable choice that must be made, friends often recognize this simultaneously and can part ways amicably. When that's the case, it's clearly right for both parties. With other friends, it may be necessary to be more forthright and say, "I'm sorry; this just isn't working for me." That's all right too. Both options are practical, responsible choices when a relationship must come to an end. Sometimes in friendship letting go, saying goodbye, and moving on is simply a natural part of life.

When to Seek Further Help

If you are facing constant obstacles in your friendships, or differences are a source of ongoing conflict, don't wrestle with it alone. Seek help from a professional counselor or therapist who can help you sort through choices, options, and coping skills if you have any of the following behaviors or concerns on a persistent basis:

Behavior checklist:

- Anger
- Confusion
- Despair
- Difficulties making or keeping friends
- Loneliness
- Repeated conflicts
- Sadness
- Social isolation

Soul Solutions

As you seek God at this time, hear the encouraging word of the Lord to Jeremiah: "Call to me and I will answer you and I will tell you great and mighty things you do not know" (Jer. 33:3).

God's will for your life and His plan for you will evolve, including through the friends He places in your life. Friends influence your life, whether for the short or long term. God has miraculous ways of bringing people together who compliment one another. Even in friendships where obstacles exist, opportunities remain for growth, transformation, and restoration.

God provides the perfect model for overcoming barriers between people. Not only can obstacles serve a purpose in developing further understanding between friends, but they are a reminder of your alliance with God and your need for Him. Your relationship grows in the realization that you can't do it without Him. Recognizing the purpose that obstacles play in your life will be made known in God's time. He loves without fail. He asks that you do the same and trust in His wisdom and guidance.

Prayer Guide

As you turn to God in prayer, be reminded of how He will meet you right where you are as you face certain obstacles in friendships. Close your eyes for a few minutes, and seek God and His loving-kindness. The Lord will help you wash away any frustrations, loneliness, or confusion. He is able to help you overcome troubled relationships and discover opportunities within them.

Friendships, and the desire to maintain them, consistently require you to look inward, to those things within your soul that are only shared with God. Be assured that God offers freedom from the obstacles that hinder friendships; He will guide you to peace-filled decisions. He often uses difficulties to develop character, helping us to become more like Him. God's character embodies the fruit of the spirit; love, joy, peace, patience, kindness, goodness, faithfulness, self control, gentleness, and self-control (Galatians 5:22-23). As these and other beneficial characteristics are extended to others, the return to you will likely be twofold.

Remember, God can create unity in the midst of any diversity. He calms the waves!

What frustrations are you currently struggling with? Once these are clear, and you feel God's peace and confirmation, close your eyes and begin by expressing gratitude for a friend or friends. Ask God to equip you to find victory by overcoming obstacles in the battle for godly relationships. Ask for wisdom in discerning what can be changed and insight to realize what cannot. Pray for peace and guidance in your decision-making and be reminded that He is always in control. Ask to be receptive to what God says; then respond.

What you can do:

- Pray about the specific obstacle. Ask for what you hope to happen, remembering to accept the outcome. Know God hears, though His timing may be different from yours. As you seek His guidance, be receptive to a fresh perspective and attitude.
- Be open to seeing the opportunities that God might show you within this challenge. Remember nothing is new to Him. With God's influence, the possibilities and positive outcomes are often beyond what you might ever expect.
- Look forward to positive growth and change within yourself and your attitudes as God helps you adapt to any change.
- After praying or reading Scripture, sit quietly. Enjoy the solitude.
- Pray for the ability to exhibit the fruits of the spirit as you face challenging obstacles.

Spending time with God in prayer and His Word will enlighten you much more than any words written on this page. May you find His abundant goodness in your friendships today.

Closing Scripture

Each week consider one verse you want to put into action and attitude. Take note of how these critical qualities make a difference in your relationships.

> *A time to search and time to give up as lost; a time to keep and a time to throw away. A time to tear apart, and a time to sew together; a time to be silent, and a time to speak* (Ecclesiastes 3: 6-7).

> *Make every effort to keep the unity of the Spirit through the bond of peace (*Ephesians 4:3 NIV).

> *Tribulation produces perseverance; and perseverance, character; and character, hope* (Romans 5:3-4 NKJV).

Friend-to-Friend Activities

1. **Send a Revolving Card**

Across the miles, (or across the street), stay connected with a card that returns every Christmas, birthday, holiday, every month, or New Year. Mail it back and forth. When it's your turn to send it, add a line of inspiration, news, prayer, or wishes to keep your friendship active and up to date. This idea came from Loretta and Jerri (both age 79). For more than 50 years they sent one large Christmas card back and forth, alternating the years from California to Minnesota and back again. The card was covered with dates and messages. Their children loved the idea and their example served to inspire this special practice with friends. Not only is the card part of Loretta and Jerri's friendship history, but today it's also a collector's item.

2. **Art Collage**

One way to stay connected and honor the differences

between you and a friend is to make a collage that illustrates your lives together. It's fun and simple. Begin by cutting out images, colors, words, and pictures from magazines, newspapers, and ads that represent who you are individually and what you share in common as friends. Paste your cutouts on a card, box, poster, or any size paper suitable for framing. Make it personal and meaningful to your lives and personalities. This is a project that is a one-of-a-kind creation and is as distinctive as your friendship.

3. **"I'm Hopeful..."**

List one friend or more and think about the hope you have for them, and for yourself, regarding an obstacle that stands between you. How have you been encouraged, guided, or influenced by what you have read in this chapter? Jot down a note to yourself. Picture what you might do differently to enhance your relationship with friends, in your desire and hope for long-term friendship.

4. **Standing In Her Shoes**

You may choose to do this alone or with a friend. Imagine you are your friend. Stand in her shoes and experience life completely from her standpoint. Describe yourself in detail as if you were her, beginning in "I am . . ." statements. Describe looks (color of eyes, hair, skin, etc.), factual information (where she lives, works, who her family consists of, etc.), and describe her religion, beliefs, and how she approaches life. Describe what makes her laugh, cry, and what she feels passionate about and why. Now explain her most challenging obstacle related to being your friend. Talk about how she might feel and what she needs in order to resolve this with you. Repeat the exercise having your friend stand in your shoes. Now discuss and ask yourselves the following: What did you learn or discover about one another that you may not have appreciated or been aware of before? How will this help you face the obstacle(s) in your friendship?

Chapter 3

Anguish

> Now that I know something is wrong between us, I'm more than stunned. I can't say this to you partly because I can't seem to put words on the agonizing emotions that are churning, but I guess this sums it up: I feel like I've been fired as your soul mate.
> — *Sally (age 51)*

The loss of a friend is a harsh reality; it hurts. When the ties of a connected and valuable relationship are severed even temporarily, the results can be devastating. Anguish between friends can spring from hurtful actions or circumstances. Coping with the fallout of painful events can be complicated and challenging.

The emotional transparency close friends share can build strong and faithful bonds. When women hold a spoken and unspoken trust and understanding, exposing secrets and painful life experiences to one another is natural. When you have confidence that friends hold your best interests at heart, it's natural to expose personal vulnerabilities and weaknesses. In this trusting climate, a sense of safety is fostered, and it's easy to believe the friendship can endure almost anything. However, if the sharing and caring between friends has shifted or is not reciprocated, problems arise.

When someone gets burned, bitterness and resentment threaten to extinguish even the best of relationships.

A number of factors can influence the way you respond to hurt and conflict in friendships. Your upbringing and relationship history set the stage for how you tend to react to problems. Personality traits and expectations also influence the degree of anguish you may experience in difficult situations. Regardless, most women say the confusion from a sudden hostility or an abrupt change in attitude can cause great suffering. The distress can quickly put a friendship on trial, testing its limits.

For friends who usually think alike, misunderstandings and opposing perspectives are more than an unwelcome surprise. Mary (age 38) described a serious disagreement she experienced with a close friend. She said:

> Until this happened, we were able to finish each other's sentences. Now I don't have a clue what she is thinking, and she doesn't understand me either. It's so out of character for us . . . strange really, but mostly sad.

Most women aren't wired to forget hurt easily, and many admit they stew over the details longer than they'd like. Loss of a close friend or adjusting to a significant change in a relationship can set off a grieving process just as a divorce or other loss might. Women say the whole experience is often accompanied by repeated efforts to make concessions and frequent attempts to gain understanding of the problem. Anguish can stem from any number of situations between friends. One common challenge is passive distancing, or feeling ignored. Other painful situations include outright betrayal or pressure stemming from unrealistic expectations and competitiveness. Uncomfortable feelings of envy or jealousy also contaminate relationships. Women experience great torment when friendships abruptly end or a friend is lost due to death. Whatever the scenario, the grief can be palpable when friends become a mere memory. It's a testing time as the outward hurt forces deep, inner examination.

Emotional Loss

As best friends and soul mates for more than 30 years, Sally and her friend shared everything in life. As the opening quote explains, Sally's loss was an emotional one. When her friend suddenly started relating to her as a casual acquaintance and pulled away emotionally, Sally was devastated. Trust and confidence were compromised. Their strong friendship took a shocking new direction. Sally said she never imagined in her wildest dreams that she would have a story to contribute to this book, let alone to the chapter focused on "anguish." She asked:

> I wonder how many women out there are like me? How many are filled with sadness and regret when they think of a cherished friend who, without notice or obvious cause, just seems to slip away . . . maybe not physically, but emotionally there is a disconnect. If I permanently lose this friend, it will be very hard to deal with. The person I thought I knew seems to have disappeared before my eyes.

It's easy and comfortable to assume a longtime friendship you believe in will remain a positive and constant source of security. Many friendships do remain stable and secure, but many more do not. Countless women say they have grappled with a profound sense of heartache related to friends, not unlike Sally's experience. They didn't believe a wedge could ever come between them, until it did.

During this difficult crossroad, Sally wrote this to her friend in a journal entry:

> How does this happen to two friends who love each other and have been through decades of life together? Sometimes change is good, and I'm open to that possibility, but what good change is happening here? The sorrow, pain, and frustration just won't go away. It's raw grief. I know it sounds dramatic given all the problems in this world, but it is big—this is about one of the most important relationships in my life! I keep thinking, "I'm a mature woman, get a grip." I keep grasping for who you've always been to me, but you're not acting the same towards me. When we try to talk, we just circle around each other. Your words and actions conflict, and I feel there is something you just can't tell me. What's the problem? Each time I struggle to make sense of the rejection I feel from you, I'm filled with absolute shock and disbelief all over again. I wonder if it will ever be straightened out. I haven't experienced a divorce, but it must feel something like this.

Solutions

It's hard to accept when the one friend you thought you could always trust and depend on let's you down. Anita (age 37) said:

> Loss of trust is loss of everything. It's the foundation for relationships. Without it, the deep bond you once shared with that person never returns, and it's hopeless. I know because it happened to me, and I had to just walk away. I wonder if there's something more we could have done to save our friendship. I regret

not trying, but we just gave up and it still kills me inside.

Sometimes walking away from a friendship is the only course of action that can be taken. You may need to fondly remember the good times and move forward. However, the challenges presented within friendships provide opportunities when they are faced candidly and honestly. Regardless of the outcome, one thing is certain—anguish will not go away until you do something about it.

It's not easy to rebuild a shattered friendship, but it's possible when friends hold the mutual goal of restoring hope and confidence in their relationship. Many women say overcoming emotional hurt and conflict in their friendships have added depth of character and a renewed sense of meaning to their relationship. If both individuals desire the same outcome, friendships cannot only survive adversity; they can also grow stronger through it.

It's encouraging to recognize how the power of a loving friendship can survive almost anything. For many people the influence of a friend remains even following their death. There is a reason that Paul reminds of the strength and importance of love in I Corinthians 13:13. He says, "But now faith, hope, love, abide in these three; but the greatest of these is love."

Love and forgiveness aren't always easy or natural human responses, but they are the key to resolving hurt and disappointment. Even when forgiveness doesn't bring reconciliation or mend a broken relationship, the act of forgiveness frees you. It makes way for your own peace and healing. Forgiveness doesn't mean forgetting because past events remain unchanged. But forgiveness does mean accepting and remembering, finding a place in yourself where the anguish can be put to rest once and for all. As you rely on your faith to help you do this, God also expects you to assume personal responsibility for doing what is within your power about a situation.

Marti (age 40) said:

> In my opinion, prayer isn't the solution to everything. God gave us a brain to think with and the ability to make choices. We shouldn't pray without also taking direct action to do something about our problems.

It takes courage and loyalty to forgive and rebuild trust. The first step begins by accepting the fact that you're angry or saddened by a friend's actions. Learning to confront the problem head-on with straightforward communication and honesty are the next steps.

Anger Can Be Positive

Anger is a God-given emotion. Everyone has it and everyone feels it. Most people are challenged to manage anger appropriately under certain conditions and in some situations. Many women say they are not comfortable with anger no matter what the reason and have a difficult time expressing it. Others equate anger with rejection. Some say they avoid it by stuffing angry feelings down, or like a pressure cooker they blow up when the steam builds to a point where it can no longer be contained. Either way, anger can't be denied.

Anger does not have to be negative, and it's not always a sin. In fact, anger can be a dynamic and powerful expression of what is decent and true. It can change bad situations for the good. History shows how anger has been the impetus for bringing bad to good; in some cases it is a sure sign of moral integrity.

When expressed in healthy ways, anger can be a tool in

friendship too. It can help friends focus on problems that need to be confronted. It can lead to new awareness that opens the door for greater understanding and trust. However, when anger controls someone or is used as a weapon of revenge, it can confuse, complicate, and distort the issues at hand. Unhealthy anger hurts, while healthy anger is fair and productive.

Anger may be a consequence of not confronting problems soon enough, or not taking time to think about what emotional wounds might be driving it. It's important to note that there is always hurt underneath anger. When friends are in conflict, focusing on the injury rather than the rage can be helpful. Understanding that you have hurt underneath the anger is the quickest way to diffuse it.

What you can do

- Remember, anger can be a natural and beneficial emotion between friends. Expressing this emotion doesn't have to mean rejection or the end of a friendship.
- Don't judge whether your friend should or shouldn't be feeling angry. The fact is that her perspective needs to be respected.
- Learn to clearly identify when you are angry. Pay attention to physical sensations you are aware of such as a racing heart, clenched jaw, flushed skin, or shaky hands. Become familiar with specific thoughts and the emotional experiences that accompany or ignite your anger.
- Take responsibility for feeling the way you do. Acknowledge anger when you have it; accept it and own it. For example, "I can admit I am angry right now. This is how I feel."
- Ask yourself what hurt you might be experiencing underneath your anger. What might you be afraid of or what is

causing your frustration? What and who has hurt you?

- Find creative and productive outlets for your anger. You might work out, clean, write, talk it through, take a walk, or breathe and relax.
- Prevent unhealthy expressions of anger by communicating thoughts and feelings as they arise. Don't let negative attitudes accumulate and fester. Instead, open up and speak your mind through your heart. Learning positive confrontation skills can help you find ways to do this effectively.

The Art of Confrontation

There is an art to confronting a sensitive situation with a friend without fear of ruining the relationship. If you're like many, even the idea of staging a confrontation with a friend sounds like a recipe for disaster. The idea that an unsettled disagreement may have to be re-hashed can create strong feelings of anxiety and vulnerability for women. Some worry they will explode in anger or tears and that it will end in more pain. Most fear confrontation will only make matters worse.

It's challenging to exercise assertiveness when conflict is something you want to avoid rather than deal with. Some women dread it so much they think discarding a friendship is easier than facing a conflict openly and honestly. Learning to confront problems rather than people can help save a valuable friendship. Frank discussion is necessary, and without it, a friendship is likely to spiral downward fast.

Confrontation is not always pain-free or comfortable. Sharing difficult, private feelings is always tough. Feelings of anxiety and fear are common when dealing with someone you have a problem with.

Everyone experiences either a fight or flight physiological response in reaction to stressful events they perceive to be frightening or dangerous. Typically, fears are dispelled once discussions get going. When talking things out together in a constructive and loving way, the process will eventually serve to calm you both rather than ignite further conflict. Anxiety is usually diminished or alleviated entirely by expressing your true thoughts and feelings.

Confronting rifts and the feelings involved takes practice, but it gets easier with time. The benefits usually outweigh the transitory discomfort that confrontation creates for many women. To help you cope with tension and manage your physical responses to stress, practice the breathing exercises and stress reduction skills described in Chapter One. Then, take direct action utilizing the steps below. The suggestions are based on therapeutic strategies to help you successfully confront a problem or painful situation with a friend.

Remember, Scripture also directs people to deal with problems in a constructive and agreeable way. All of us are instructed to talk privately together about disagreements or wrongs, and to avoid gossip and public confrontations. It's important to sit down together and take Apostle Paul's words to heart; appeal to your friend in faith, hope, and love.

What you can do:

- First, pray and give thanks for your friend. (Refer to Soul Solutions at the end of this chapter for help with spiritual guidelines.)
- Be clear about your feelings, motivations, and purpose before talking to the person.
- Pick a convenient, undistracted time and place that suits both of you.
- Commit to an honest discussion and agree to stay on track.

• Use statements that begin with "I…" instead of "You…" "I" statements minimize defensiveness and language that may sound or feel attacking.

• Be willing to listen to one another's needs and perspectives without interruption. Some find it helpful to set a timer for 15 minutes and speak freely without interruption while the other listens attentively.

• Repeat back to your friend what you hear them saying and vice versa. Check the accuracy of what you heard.

• Go back and clarify with one another any areas in which you want or need further understanding. Again, take turns doing this and do not interrupt one another as each clarifies information and feelings further.

• Admit your part in the problem.

• Confront the problem, not your friend.

• Be sincere and honest.

• Speak first-hand knowledge; use specific examples and stick to the facts.

• Remind yourself that you cannot change other people, but you can change yourself. You don't have to prove yourself right. Instead, you can agree to disagree.

• Sometimes it's best to focus on reconciliation of the relationship rather than resolution of the problem. It's great to have both when you can, but if that's not possible, make it a goal to put the well-being of your relationship first.

• Remember, reconciliation is a mutual process. It's not always a fifty-fifty proposition the whole way through but it's something that needs to be faced by both individuals every step of the way.

When Unrealistic Expectations Create Problems

Right or wrong, women hold expectations for one another. Emotional hurts from the past and present as well as perceived needs can contribute to the kinds of expectations you hold. Every friend is unique and probably expects different things in different ways. For instance, some women expect quality time with friends on a regular and consistent basis. Regular lunch dates or late night chats might be two ways to find meaningful time together. Others expect to hear they are valued verbally through the words spoken to them, for example: "You're a great friend" or "You are so important to me." Still others expect help and assistance with various tasks like helping with a garage sale or painting a room in order to know someone cares. Some friends expect to give and receive gifts or cards in order to feel special. Many women need physical touch and affection to feel connected to their friends, while others say they aren't the "touchy-feely" type at all.

It's vital to be aware of how you communicate care for friends and to know what you need from friends in return. What may be an unrealistic expectation from your point of view may feel like an absolute necessity for someone else.

When a friend doesn't feel her needs have been met, she may feel hurt or let down. She may not recognize how her expectations place pressure and demands on friends. Janie (age 34) felt overwhelmed by what a friend wanted from her. She said, "I just can't meet all the expectations she has for me. I seem to fail every time, and it's overwhelming! I'd prefer not to be 'needed' at all."

Pamela (age 47) explained the problem of unrealistic expectations from her perspective:

> I'm easygoing and I have no expectations for my friends except for this: my friends must love me more than they need me. If they need me too much, I will only be a disappointment. My friends are independent with strong egos. I don't have the time, energy, or patience for those who grow insecure with the limits my busy life imposes. When expectations become too high, or just too much, I feel smothered. I have to step out for air and literally back away. The fact is, I cannot be available to a girlfriend on a consistent basis; my life does not allow it. I don't allow it. I can't be needed more than loved, or it absolutely will not work.

It's likely to drive friends away when women create demands and place unrealistic expectations on their friends. However, sometimes the person with high expectations drives herself away first. Some women give up or bail out of a friendship after feeling personally let down from unmet expectations. Either way, it's a losing situation for both individuals as illustrated in the following situation:

> Jen was my first real friend when I moved here. We were close for years and shared a lot in common. The only difference between us was that I was working full-time and had to work extra to make ends meet.
>
> I still can't say for certain what caused our friendship to end so abruptly. One day I ran into her at the store while shopping with my daughter. I was excited to see her and told her I had been thinking about her and wanting to call. She looked surprised and offended at the same time. She told me she had to go and walked away. Just like that. I stood frozen

for a moment feeling like a rope had just wrapped around my insides. My daughter looked at me and said solemnly, "Mom, you have just been dumped." And she was right.

That was nearly seven years ago. I spent the first couple years obsessing off and on about what I had done wrong, wondering if it was because I didn't call her enough, or because she felt I didn't care enough. It seemed to me her expectations for our friendship were different from mine. I have concluded that I unintentionally hurt her because of what she expected from me and what I expected from her. I thought we understood one another, but I guess not. After all this time it still feels sad to me. I miss her. But it was clear when the door slammed in my face that she was done. I just had to accept that I couldn't give whatever it was she needed. *—Meg (age 44)*

Losing friends without the chance for mutual understanding or reconciliation is difficult. Being suddenly avoided or treated rudely hurts. Keep in mind though, people tend to re-enact on others what's been done to them. Ironically, the way friends behave towards you might be the way they believe you've behaved towards them. Another possibility is that it has nothing to do with you or what you have or haven't done. A friend's reactions may not be intentional or even conscious. They may stem from personal wounds in childhood or frequent disappointments with others throughout life. Sometimes indifference and rejection become an expectation in and of itself. People often create what they anticipate, and when they do, actions of anger or detachment rather than reconciliation can be the result.

At times a lack of self-confidence and self-esteem can

cause some women to set their expectations too low. They may accept friends into their lives who do not give and take in a mutually caring way.

Melody (age 33) described a family member who had such low self-worth that she settled for whatever any friend was willing to give her, even when that friend took advantage of her. She said:

> It's hard to see someone I care about not being assertive enough. Women need to exercise their right and ability to verbalize their true thoughts and feelings to friends without fear of ridicule, shame, or rejection. And if it results in a painful outcome, then I say get out of that relationship, and get out fast. My sister deserves better, but she settles for less all the time. She doesn't expect to be treated well, and so guess what? She isn't treated well. I'm sad to say, she would do better with a Golden Retriever for a friend. At least they are loyal and loving.

It's been said that when there are no expectations there can be no disappointments. However, healthy expectations are essential to lasting relationships. They help define who you are and what you need. In this way, to expect is to be hopeful. It's evidence of self-worth. Like Melody's sister, when you live without any expectations, you are likely to feel invisible and without influence. You may be forever vulnerable to the whims of others. As long as expectations are considerate and realistic, they can be assertively communicated and mutually accepted. In this way, healthy expectations can be constructive and empowering in friendships.

Communicating your differences in outlooks up front can save you a colossal amount of grief. Understanding expectations held between friends can be a crucial first step to preventing misunderstandings. Employing strategies early on in friendships is the first step to preventing eruptions of mayhem because of mismatched needs. Explore some or all of the following issues with friends to help clarify the expectations you each see as necessary and unnecessary in your relationships.

What you can do:

• Think about what you anticipate gaining from a friendship. If it helps, make a list of what you long to receive from friends, and what you desire to give. Discuss these together. Right away, this may prevent or pinpoint an area of conflict.

• From each of your viewpoints, talk about specific actions and behaviors you perceive as hurtful. Discuss what actions and behaviors are helpful in maintaining your friendship.

• Be forthright. Agree to directly discuss your lifestyle and personality differences. Compare your needs. This understanding may immediately bring more mutual acceptance.

• Think about the amount of time you can spend with friends and prepare them for the limits you might have. For instance, how easily can you respond to a friend's needs when stressed or already over-committed? Share and listen.

• What do your friends need to know about you? When it comes to personality quirks and behaviors, talk about what friends should know about you. For example, you could share, "Don't take it personally if I can't call you regularly. I'm less regimented and more spontaneous. My friends need to know that about me."

• To avoid hurt feelings or confusion, you might want to agree on how you will or will not acknowledge special occasions like birthdays and holidays. This is more important for some than others. Reach an understanding between you. For example, "For me, our friendship does not depend on receiving or sending cards. Are you okay with that?"

- Talk about special things friends have done that made you feel especially cared about. This confirms the good elements already happening in your relationships.
- Consider what expectations of yours might stem from strengths and weaknesses in your personality or past experiences. For example, "Because I grew up feeling I had to be perfect, I tend to expect the same from others." Or, "Sometimes I forget my sense of humor and outlook on life aren't always shared or appreciated in the way I expect. Bear with me!"
- Think about the expectations you hold that might be driven by past or present circumstances or insecurities rather than something your friend has done. Discuss.
- Be aware that most friends have at least some different needs. Remain true to yourselves. Acknowledge that you won't do everything the same. Acceptance paves the way for true friendship.

I Hate to Admit It, but I'm Jealous

Some emotional challenges are particularly insidious and menacing. Jealousy appears to be one of them. "Don't sit under the apple tree with anyone else but me..." is from an old song that most people still recognize today. Everyone wants to feel important and special to at least one person. The same drive that causes a woman to eagerly search for that special, one and only romantic mate, can also cause her to seek a friend who will give her the title, "best friend."

Jealousy is a natural enough emotion, but it can also quickly destroy a friendship. Webster's Dictionary describes jealousy as "feeling resentment because of another's success or advantage; suspicious fears, envious resentment; vigilant in guarding."

Supposedly mature at this point, baby-boomers admit that it can be embarrassing when jealousy rears its ugly head in adult friendships.

Doris (age 49) admitted she had pangs of jealousy and resented herself for it. She said:

> Honestly, you'd think I was still in Junior High! I confess that I wanted to see and repeatedly hear I was my best friend's "best friend." There is something satisfying about knowing I'm as special to her as she is to me. Not only a best friend, but I needed to be the "very bestest." The intellectual side of me understands this is immature, simple-minded, and silly. I mean, come on...I have several friends that are so close I consider each of them a best friend in their own way. It's impossible to compare one to another. Each holds a place in my life that can be filled by no other. But I admit it; I still want to hear that I'm this friend's favorite.

No one has a friendship or a life that is identical to another. Just like the DNA that holds a body together, everyone you meet is a one-of-a-kind design. Since there can never be an exact likeness, a great variety of friends can hold a unique and special position in each other's lives in a way no other can. Discovering new best friends is like having children. It's one of the miracles of life. The love you feel for one is never diminished by the addition of others. Adding more friends simply means you have repeated opportunities to add more love to your life.

What you can do:

• Recognize jealousy in yourself. It's dangerous and prevents you from bringing out the best in yourself and your friendships.

• Ask yourself, "What specifically makes me jealous?" Admit your feelings out loud to help you gain a healthy perspective and let go of irrational or senseless feelings.

• Be aware that jealousy can be a red flag for unequal expectations between friends. Examine and re-evaluate your expectations.

• Laugh about it! Feeling jealous is truly like being in Junior High again. Admit it and begin to take yourself less seriously.

• Change your self-talk about jealousy. For example, rather than say, "I have to feel like I'm number one all the time or I can't be happy" say, "I like it when I am, but I don't have to be number one to be happy or know our friendship is real and worthwhile to me."

• Persistent insecurities can be destructive to friendships. Feeling inadequate can drive jealous feelings and serve to push others away from you. Pay attention to your self-esteem and keep it in check in order to enjoy satisfying friendships.

• Don't lose sight of yourself; live your own life. If you spend too much time second-guessing your importance in a relationship or worrying about what a friend thinks of you, you are not respecting yourself. You deserve to be special to someone without having to go through any mental anguish.

• Ask yourself why it's difficult to feel special unless you have your friend's acceptance and reassurance. Think about your past relationships as well as recent experiences. What patterns of jealousy or other insecurities have you seen in your friendships over time? It can be helpful to discuss this with a trusted friend or objective person. Remember, finding acceptance from others is nice, but you don't need it from everyone to be a happy and worthwhile friend to others.

• Remember, most people feel insecure from time to time. This feeling is common, but once understood and acknowledged, insecurity can be redirected. Focus on caring for and rewarding yourself, rather than depending on friends to do so.

• Don't give power to feelings of jealousy and they won't wreak havoc in your life.

• Most of all, find your sense of worth in God, not your friends. For further help with this, read Chapters Five and Eight.

Envy and Competition

Jealousy is not always something you feel towards others but can just as easily be something others feel towards you. And it's not just about competition with your friends. Jealousy may infect relationships through envy towards a certain lifestyle or talent. The family you enjoy or the success you've found might be a source of resentment for others. Even good luck is sometimes secretly despised by friends. Comparing your lot in life with someone else's is a sure way to perpetuate unhappiness and lose friends.

Odetta said, "The better we feel about ourselves, the fewer times we have to knock someone else down to feel tall." Sherie (age 54) has at times noticed a less than supportive atmosphere among women. She said:

> It never ceases to amaze me how many times I've witnessed women undermining one another. Not just in the work place, but in social situations, in close friendships, and even within the church. Rather than offering support and finding opportunities to build one another up, some women seem truly intent on

> bringing other women down for a fall. I've often wondered why . . . I just don't understand it except to assume that maybe these women feel so unsure about themselves that they need to make sure other women look weaker than them. I guess it's just a skewed way to feel more important.

Marilyn (age 74) believes age may make a difference. She said, "I have met women who have said that as they aged their friendships have deepened, and were not as competitive." Shirley (age 71) agreed:

> I think that as we age, all the hard, painful stuff gets easier to navigate. I certainly feel at this point in life all my friends are more secure in accepting who I am and in knowing who they are. At some point, it becomes pointless to compare yourself with anyone else. Their life may not be as ideal as it looks on the outside, anyway.

It's preferable to learn this sooner rather than later. Someone is always going to have more or less than you do. If you decide you must prove yourself by trying to be better than others, you may adopt a sense of unhealthy pride and arrogance. If you see yourself as less than others, self-depreciation and anger can easily follow. Either way, comparing yourself to friends is a no-win situation.

If you have a friend who struggles to compete with you or seems to have a deep need to be better than you, consider sharing your own feelings of inadequacy with her. Sometimes shedding light on personal insecurities can help a friend face hers. If you are met with resistance or anger, know that envy and jealousy will take no better course in your life than an unhealthy virus would—it will eventually be toxic to the relationship. If that's the direction you and a friend are headed, it may be best to count your marbles and go home. Not all friends will be in the same place as you are, and some may not be ready or capable of relating in a healthy way. Stay kind and friendly, but move on and realize people have to want to change before they can work together to find solutions.

Betrayal

Elizabeth (age 52) said, "The worst let down I ever experienced happened when a close friend betrayed my confidence using deeply private information against me." There is nothing quite like the experience of discovering that a once loyal friend can no longer be trusted. Betrayal manifests itself in many ways, and the hurt and distress it causes is like no other. In any form, friendship aggression can be especially toxic. At the very least, the friendship turns awkward; and at the very worst, it's irreversibly damaged.

Not all friendships can be repaired following a betrayal. Maybe not all friendships should. But when they can be set right, the results can make an extraordinary difference in the life of your friendship. Henry Ward Beecher said, "Every man should have a fair-sized cemetery in which to bury the faults of his friends." His idea is a good one; however, when an emotional injury is severe, it may require some time to recover before the faults of your friend can be laid to rest.

The Recovery Process

When the news or recognition of betrayal becomes apparent, the impact can be heartbreaking. Your assumptions about the person you thought you knew so well and the friendship you shared may be shattered. Most people have a stress-filled reaction to such news and feel unable to think clearly or stay balanced. Thoughts and feelings may take a roller coaster ride, and the pain that can result may feel outright unbearable.

Relationship betrayal is not unlike other traumas, and in some cases does qualify as a trauma in every clinical sense of the word. Several similarities are present between the process of recovering from an acute traumatic experience and recovering from an important person's betrayal. First, there is the shock of learning about the deed or act that has offended you. The impact of the news may bring immediate feelings of repeated denial in statements like, "There must be some mistake" or, "This can't be happening . . . not to us." Or, "I just can't believe she feels this way or would do this."

Sally continues to describe what she experienced with her close friend and soul mate:

> As adults and longtime friends, we've collectively learned so many hard lessons together. We understand the value of relationships. We know friendship and life is very fragile; how it can, and should never be taken for granted. The bond forged through our many life experiences together has only strengthened our relationship with each passing year. It makes the rejection and sense of betrayal I've experienced from her all the more perplexing. I can't quit asking, "Why is this happening to us?"

When trying to make sense of something so confusing, on-going symptoms of anxiety and depression are typical. Feelings of guilt are likely to be troublesome too. It may be difficult to shut off the thoughts and feelings inside as you repeatedly mull over the details and desperately seek answers for what went wrong.

Finally, a person can reach a stage of acceptance to what

happened. The negative events of yesterday can be replaced by hope in what is happening in the relationship today. You can forgive and reorganize your friendship around what happened, or try to come to some other form of resolution.

If the friendship is salvageable, finding a new normal can be one form of resolution. If it's not salvageable, the solution may be to recognize the damage cannot be undone. Resolution does not always mean the relationship is fixed or back to the way it was previously. It may mean you have learned to accept it has changed and acknowledge it can never be exactly the same way again.

What you can do:

- Understand there is no right or wrong way to feel following a loss of trust and betrayal.
- Accept that you will experience a wide range of reactions. Seek out support. Find someone who can listen objectively and help you sort through painful thoughts and feelings. It's been said, "What you can't put to words, you can't put to rest." Talking about what happened can help diminish the negative impact of the experience.
- Be patient with yourself and don't make any sudden decisions regarding your friendship. You may live to regret ending your relationship permanently or prematurely. Painful experiences are hard to assimilate. Time and patience are vital to come to some form of resolution and understanding about what steps, if any, can be taken next.
- As much as possible, maintain a calm attitude. A peaceful heart helps you see solutions more clearly.
- Again, remember that there is always hurt underneath anger. Ask yourself what specifically hurt you, or what was most hurtful about the betrayal.
- Keep a daily personal journal to express the full range of your thoughts and feelings.

• Explore whether or not what happened was intentional. Was your friend's behavior typical of who you know her to be? If not, consider what she intended and generously offer her leniency.

• Think about what would need to happen in order for your trust to be restored. Share this with your friend and see if a mutual commitment can be made to work towards that goal. Discuss or write a letter expressing what needs to happen for healing to occur.

• Betrayal changes you. It's not likely to make you better or worse over time, just different.

• No one can forget intentional or unintentional malice, but you can accept the faults in your friend just as you accept your own faults.

• Make the decision to forgive. Even when it's one-sided, forgiveness can be a healthy step for you. It doesn't always mend a shattered friendship, but it drapes the heart in healing.

Today, Sally and her friend are working towards honestly sharing what they feel. After some time, Sally's friend recognized what was at the root of her reactions and the reason she emotionally distanced herself from their friendship. She wrote this:

> Sally and I see what happened very differently, and we've accepted that. We both felt hurt and confused. She felt rejected and I disappeared, but only because I wanted the hurt to go away. I retreated because in the beginning I didn't know what was wrong either! But this is what it boiled down to for me: people have always told Sally and I how much we acted and looked alike. Sometimes we felt like carbon copies of one another because we are so much alike. We've

> been told that for so many years that we've always expected to feel the same about everything too. For the first time in decades, I didn't. Like sisters who are very close, I feel that we over-identified with one another. During this stage of my life, I realized I wanted my own identity, especially in an area in which we ministered together. It's evident now this need I had to feel like a separate person was at the root of our difficulties. And I'm grateful that we love each other enough to continue to fight for our friendship.

Today, Sally's relationship with her friend is solid again, though altered. The experience has shifted their friendship into a new and different place, and both women remain hopeful that the restoration will continue. Sally concluded by saying:

> I've been on my knees frequently to God, asking for help to do what I've had a hard time doing . . . to not be prideful or proven right in the situation. I've spent enough time scrutinizing myself. Now I'm moving on and not allowing bitterness to fester. I've fully forgiven, but at times I remember and I regret the sense of something lost between us. It's helped me though, now that I have a better understanding of the personal needs that were driving her actions. Today I'm making a choice to love her because I cannot imagine my life without her. God also instructs me to do this, and in doing so I believe He also supplies the sincerity of heart to put it into action. Through all of this I've realized that I can be okay with or without her support and the carefree intimacy we once shared; although for now, this has changed the depth

of our friendship. It's a tough journey to arrive at this place of acceptance of her choices, but I believe I am finally there. I feel God is using this for His purposes for me . . . and I hope for her too.

When the Offender Is You

Linda's story is different. She did not write about being betrayed; instead she shared her memory of being the betrayer. Now 52, Linda confessed her experience of having made the terrible mistake of hurting a friend nearly twenty years ago:

> Whenever you listen to or participate in gossip, it never goes down a good road. I learned the hard way. I still don't know quite how all this happened, but I made the mistake of revealing information from one friend to another that I shouldn't have. The information was used against my friend in a cruel way, and she learned that I had been the source. We talked about it a couple times, and she said she forgave me. But it wasn't the case; she never really trusted me again and who could blame her? She stopped all contact. I'll never forget something she said to me: "I just don't understand how such a smart woman could do such a stupid thing." She was right. I was smarter than that. I lost her as a friend because of it. It's one of those horrible moments I wish I could go back in time and fix! I got caught being mean, and I hurt her. I had to accept that I failed her, and the only thing left for me to do was rest in the knowledge that I would never repeat the same mistake. This was definitely a low point in the course of my human development, and it did not go unheeded. I was given a lesson. And boy, did I learn it.

What you can do

• If you've made a mistake and hurt a friend, admit the wrong to her and immediately do what you can to make it right. Talk directly to her about it, not to others.

• Periodically remind the friend whom you offended what you learned from the experience and how you have changed in order to prevent the same mistake from happening again. Then ask for forgiveness.

• Remember, verbal reassurance alone is not enough; changed behavior demonstrated consistently over time is vital.

• Take responsibility for wrong behavior, but remember both friends are responsible for the outcome. You can't achieve reconciliation alone.

• If your friend decides not to continue the friendship, respect her choice and learn from your mistake.

Sometimes you can't try any harder than you already have to salvage a friendship. You can't keep trying to rebuild a bridge that does not have the structural foundation necessary to repair it. In some cases you realize the foundation was never really there from the beginning. In other cases the injury was too great for one or the other to bear. If a friendship has ended, and it's time for one or both of you to walk away from it, openly forgive one another first if you can. Refer to the Soul Solutions section in this chapter for specific spiritual guidance as you seek to forgive and restore, or make other important modifications to your friendship.

Losing a Friend Through Death

Eventually everyone loses someone they love. It's a dreaded fact of life. For some, death is complicated by deep fears and feelings of abandonment. Anxiety about death is not an uncommon experience, but it's always an unwelcome one. Losing a friend to death changes your life forever. This experience is as individual as the grief process itself. Learning to live without someone and knowing it's permanent never ceases to be sad. But like a severe trauma, the anguish can eventually be accepted and healed.

Any loss in your life brings with it a certain amount of pain and suffering. And then, out of the clear blue sky, it can transform. From grief, an unexpected sort of comfort can emerge. And within that comfort are poignant memories that can accompany and fortify you for the rest of your life.

At the age of 47, Sandra lost a friend to lung cancer. Even though they had time to say goodbye, she never felt finished saying her farewells until long after her death. Here is her story:

> Karen and I worked together for more than ten years. She was a hospice worker and death educator—an ironic fact we never quite got over when she found out she had less than a few months left to live. We met for lunch. She said she ordered the miso soup with tofu for its healing properties . . . and then laughed. Nothing seemed to make sense anymore. She coughed repeatedly with almost every breath and was waiting for radiation treatments to fix that at least.
>
> She told me she chose to spend time with me because I didn't treat her like she was dead already. And because I didn't react and cry and need her to take care of me. More than anything, she said she needed to say whatever came to mind, and she needed to be with people who could let her be herself. She explained "herself" was someone even she

didn't know anymore. Not right now anyway. I assured her I would be whatever she needed me to be, and that I would be strong. We did not share the same faith; but nevertheless, I was confident in where she was going and told her so.

In the weeks ahead we would continue to meet over steaming pots of tea, and she told me she was okay: "I'm not fine, but I want you to know, I am fine. I have accepted what is going to happen and I have peace." And then in her usual style, Karen asked me, "What do you want to know? What can I tell you about what I am going through that might help you or others?"

I said my final goodbye two days before she passed away. I had never sat at someone's death bed before, and it was unlike anything I had imagined it to be. My memory of that day is as content and peaceful now as it was then. Her room was warm and light. White sheer curtains blew in and out from a gentle breeze and exposed her spring garden in full bloom. There was peace all around us. I felt relaxation and love there. I returned home and cried for two days. With the news of her death, I cried for another few weeks . . . off and on in varying degrees of intensity.

Then it came: a letter from her. She was always expressing her appreciation and wisdom, and helping others feel okay with whatever they were going through. This letter was no exception. For a split moment, seeing her familiar handwriting made me feel she had come back. I taped it to my desk next to her picture where I often studied it, half expecting to read something new between the lines each time.

> Then one afternoon I felt her presence as strongly as if we were sitting together with our tea again. I stopped my work and went for a walk. The clouds broke apart, and when the sun hit me in just such a way, the warmth from her room came back, and I am certain she surrounded me. In that moment, I felt perfect peace and acceptance. My grief changed that day. All I know is I never felt despair again.
>
> Karen's friendship continues to serve me. The fear and sting of her loss has been replaced by all of what she left inside me. It's a continual reminder that I need to give of myself every chance I get, so the memories of me will someday serve my loved ones in this same way. I get it now when people say you carry people you love inside yourself forever. It was just a nice thing I learned to say before, but now when I say it I mean it.

In spite of the grief experienced from the death of friends, Helen Keller acknowledged the eternal benefits of friendship when she wrote: "With every friend I love who has been taken into the brown bosom of the earth, a part of me has been buried there; but their contribution to my being of happiness, strength and understanding remains to sustain me in an altered world."

Every day, life is filled with tragedy and sadness for someone. No one is immune or protected from this fact of life. Some of you know this experience only too well and perhaps have lived through ongoing or multiple tragedies throughout your life. The importance of living today, in this very minute, becomes even clearer when a friend or loved one's moments of life have been cut short. The world is ever changing and unpredictable. You need friends, as Helen Keller explained, to "sustain" you. In some small way, it can be a comforting thought to know the contributions all friends make to one another can continue, even after death.

What you can do:

- Remember death is a natural part of life, but it's only a part. Like a book, your life has many chapters in it with more yet to be written.
- As long as you are not hurting yourself or others, there is no right or wrong way to grieve. Everyone mourns at their own pace and in their own way.
- Don't be alone if you feel better being around people.
- Lower your expectations of yourself for a time. No one functions in their usual way following a loss.
- Pay attention to your grief. Find a way to let it pour out. There are benefits to allowing yourself the freedom to truly grieve so that you can truly heal.
- Express your grief for as long as it's there.
- Remember, "this too shall pass," no matter how hard the experience.
- Crying about something sad is a healthy way to release emotions.
- Find creative outlets for your grief. Create a collage or painting. Decorate a memory book or box in which to keep mementos and photos.
- Write a letter about your friend and address it to her or to God.
- Keep a journal of your thoughts and feelings as you move through each grieving experience you encounter.
- Participate in rituals or traditions you find helpful.
- Honor your friend in a ceremony or activity you create. For example, organize a prayer vigil or remembrance circle. Invite people to take turns lighting individual candles as they share a positive memory, and pass the flame around

the circle in remembrance of your friend.

• When it's your turn to comfort a grieving friend, remember what was most helpful for you. Simply be present. Your hope and encouragement for the future are usually best communicated through listening.

When To Seek Further Help

If you have difficulty coping with persistent feelings of jealousy and anger or prolonged grief, seeking additional support can be important. Feelings of low self-worth often trigger a host of insecurities in relationships. It may be beneficial to address one or more of the following concerns with a professional counselor or therapist when symptoms like those listed below are persistent, prolonged, or distressing. Also it's good to seek help if you no longer experience satisfying friendships or find it difficult to live your best each day.

Behavior checklist:

- Anxiety
- Anger or rage
- Depression, including hopelessness and despair
- Sleep disturbance
- Change in appetite
- Thoughts or acts or self-harm
- Thoughts or attempts to end your life
- Tearfulness
- Irritability
- Difficulty concentrating
- Inability to relax
- Loss of pleasure in usual activities
- Guilt feelings; regret and remorse
- Self-medicating with alcohol, drugs, or other potentially

harmful behavior such as compulsive shopping, sex, gambling, eating, etc.

- Worthlessness

Soul Solutions

God's desire is to comfort you. As written in Hebrews 4:16. "Let us draw near with confidence to the throne of grace, so that we may receive mercy and find grace to help in time of need." The quality of your connections to friends is often an indication of how deeply you are connected to God, so draw near to Him.

Sometimes anguish and sadness result from the loss of something emotionally valuable within a relationship. All loss, including betrayal or the physical death of a friend, can be a wake-up call to the level of your spiritual health. If you are separated from friends because of negative feelings or actions, you may need to ask if you are closing the door to God at that time too.

Difficult circumstances with friends always hold enormous potential for spiritual lessons and growth. However yielding to God's leading when you're upset and anxious for a swift solution to your anguish can be no easy task. Finding greater understanding for yourself and about yourself may take more time than you would like. With patience, however, God's strength of character can comfort you, moving you from hurt to healing.

At times the only answer is to hand your anguish over to God and trust He will lead you forward to a healthy outcome. You're not alone; God is faithful to restore the hurting. Sometimes you must accept the absence of an immediate fix. However, be encouraged, because harmony and healing between friends can happen in the blink of an eye and in unexpected ways that God alone can orchestrate.

Christians are called to forgive one another as we have been forgiven. Drawing strength from within brings obedience in this challenging area. Forgiving stretches and humbles as it nurtures reliance and growth in God. Best of all, the choice to forgive frees you from internal anguish.

Prayer Guide

As you turn to God, be reminded of how He will meet you right where you are in your current circumstances. Rest in solitude for a few minutes and seek God and His faithful presence to help wash away any frustration or uncertainty. He can transform hurting relationships and painful circumstances between friends. God promises to be there for you at all times and in all situations, no matter how hard. He promises to help you and never to leave or forsake you (Hebrews 13: 5-6).

What are the sources of your greatest anguish that you know about right now? Once these seem clear, seek God for fresh understanding and perspective. Close your eyes and begin by expressing gratitude for your friend. Ask to be given the tools and the sincere attitude needed to handle this uncomfortable situation successfully. Pray for peace and guidance. Be reminded that God is always in control.

What you can do:

- Pray for your friend and pray for yourself.
- Read God's Word and keep a spiritual journal. You might want to write down meaningful scriptures; note why and how they apply to you and friendship. Add prayer requests and outcomes. Reflect on any new insights and understanding you gain. A journal is also a helpful place to record your questions and feelings towards God. Remember, He can handle anything you have to say.

• Be open to seeing new things that God will show you. Let Him give guidance and increase your awareness of your own faults and shortcomings. (Pay attention to the "log" in your own eye, as referred to in the closing scripture.)

• Forgive your friend, and forgive yourself. Ask God to help you do this.

• Ask God to work in your friendship to bring about compassion, healing, and growth.

• Ask God to comfort you and restore your trust in all that is still good in life and in the relationship.

• Remember, love is stronger than anguish. Allow love to force cynicism and other negative feelings away from you.

• Ask that your friendship be transformed according to His will.

• Ask for acceptance and courage to face situations that cannot, or will not be changed.

• Pray for faith and understanding, even in times when you lose all faith and understanding.

• Be open to those individuals God may bring into your life to comfort and assist you. Allow them to give you added support.

• Above all, continually cultivate a loving heart.

The Apostle Paul implicitly acknowledges we will not be able to be at peace with everyone. But he makes it clear that if there is any room to move towards reconciliation, then we are to do so. The result is changed hearts and changed lives—for your friend and for yourself. Spending time with God in prayer and His Word will enlighten you much more than any words written on this page. May you find His goodness plentiful in your friendships today.

Closing Scripture

Each week consider one verse you want to put into action and attitude. Take note of how these critical qualities make a difference in your relationships.

> *Pursue peace . . . See to it that no one comes short of the grace of God; that no root of bitterness springing up causes trouble* (Hebrews 12:14-15).

> *Why do you look at the speck that is in your brother's eye, but do not notice the log that is in your own eye?* (Matthew 7:3)

> *Through presumption comes nothing but strife, but with those who receive counsel is wisdom* (Proverbs 13:10).

> *Be kind to one another, tender-hearted, forgiving each other, just as God in Christ also has forgiven you* (Ephesians 4:32).

> *Blessed are the peacemakers, for they shall be called sons* [daughters] *of God* (Matt. 5:9).

Friend-to-Friend Activities

Before and after you complete each of the following activities, rate your anger on a scale of one to ten ("one" being no anger, and "ten" being the most you have ever felt in your life). Which activity helped you lower your numbers on the scale? Which helped the most, and which helped the least? Continue those activities that lowered your distress.

1. **Gratitude letter:** Write a letter of gratitude to a friend you have faced a challenge with, or a friend with whom you are currently in a painful situation. Express positive feelings

only. Describe the value the friendship has to you. Share what she means to you and why you are thankful for her. Some women put this in the mail with a special card or gift, or others use this exercise as a guide for speaking directly to their friend.

2. **Forgiveness exercise**: Make a list of why you forgive an important friend. Note: Do not list what you forgive, only why. "I forgive you because …."

3. **Junior High revisited:** This activity requires a certain amount of acting, and even bad acting will be great. You and your friend will need to be at a point in your relationship where humor and fun can be appreciated again. A certain amount of healing and reconciliation should have already taken place. If you are both agreeable and ready to have fun with it, this exercise might be worth trying.

Role-play: Act out the conflict you've experienced with a friend and together re-enact it as if you were children again. Talk, complain, yell, scold, write notes, walk away, laugh, scream, and cry, but do it all from a child's point of view. Next, switch roles and try it again. It's not only silly, but this is a quick way to lighten up your issues and take the hard stuff less seriously for a while.

When you switch roles it can help you gain your friend's perspective. Your ability to role play each other also affirms your level of understanding of one another's experience. This can help as you progress through the challenging process of reconciliation. The child or young adolescent perspective may surprise you and help manifest an adult perspective sooner rather than later.

Chapter 4

Healthy Choices

> Needy women wear me out. I'm not talking about a friend in a real crisis, who may temporarily need more than the usual support. I'm talking about women who are too intense about the friendship and need constant reassurance. They are overly devoted and accompanied by a subtle sucking sound, which is all of my energy going into the black hole of their insecurity. I don't need to be that liked. *—Maureen (age 49)*

Making healthy choices in how you interact with and choose friends can mean the difference between satisfaction in relationships and total exhaustion. Friendships can fortify and uplift you spiritually, or discourage and dampen your spirit. Those that depress and wear you out, can quickly become relationships for which you sacrifice yourself. When unwise friendship choices are made, it's easy to get stuck in a downward spiral of negative behaviors. Turning around unhealthy choices and avoiding the black holes created by friends with high needs can be a heavy challenge

There are both healthy and an unhealthy ways to do just about everything in life. Good physical, emotional, and spiritual health depend on wise decisions and common sense. When you make the effort to surround yourself with people who are good for you, life can be happier and more productive. However, things get complicated when you become entangled by friends who need constant attention, demonstrate unhealthy choices, or continually struggle with serious personal problems.

If you like to save people and solve their problems, consider the high cost of rescuing others. Not only can it hurt you, it's often not the best way to help a friend. If you forged a friendship with someone who lives in a perpetual storm of problems, it may be time to learn new skills and set limits around your involvement.

Complex friendship situations can seem daunting, but they don't have to deter you from enjoying healthy relationships. Effective ways to lend a hand and direct someone in need to the right kind of support are within reach. By changing the way you relate to troubled friends, you can lessen the negative impact their situations have on you. At the same time, you can provide genuine love and support, building healthier relationships with all the friends in your life. You can effectively learn how to choose friends and avoid situations that are clearly counterproductive to your well-being.

High Maintenance Friends

As Maureen describes in the opening quote of this chapter, a clear distinction exists between a friend in a real crisis who temporarily needs more than the usual support and a friend who routinely depletes you of everything you have to give. High maintenance friends can be a lot of work; they may feel entitled to all your time and attention and expect you to drop everything to help them. No matter how busy you may be, they're not likely to recognize your limits, or care that the giving is all one-sided.

There are usually conscious and unconscious motives that drive a high maintenance friend to do what she does. Some women have experienced profound rejection or wounds so deep they will do just about anything to avoid further loss. Those who cling tenaciously to you, as well as those who habitually rescue others, may have adopted these behaviors to avoid further rejection. Overdependence on you and others is nothing more than a desperate attempt to belong and feel valued. It's natural to desire secure relationships; it's not natural to expect friends to meet all your needs.

Everyone needs to be dependent on others to some extent. Mart De Haan with Radio Bible Class (RBC) Ministries said, "On our own, we lack the variety of strengths and abilities that are necessary to keep us from being reabsorbed into a materialistic, self-centered existence." Some dependency then is natural and beneficial, but a friend who is overdependent seldom takes any responsibility for her actions and behaviors. She is frequently lonely and lacks confidence. A friend who seems to rely on others too much may want decisions made for her and is often afraid to be alone. She may need others to accompany her in order to go places and to be able to do things. She is likely to need continual affirmation to indulge her never ending neediness.

If you're an independent woman, you may resent having to deal with the insecurities and constant needs of an overly clingy friend. You also may feel like a mother or therapist instead of a friend. However, extremely independent personalities have their drawbacks too. Women who have fiercely autonomous, self-sufficient friends often complain they don't share openly enough, express needs, or give a great deal of mutual support.

Linda (age 37) said:

> I have a friend who is so independent that even when she clearly needs my support, I am not free to offer it. She pushes people away during the times she needs them most. Unfortunately I don't feel valuable to her. In my opinion, because of her fierce self-sufficiency she loses the opportunity to let her guard down, and I lose the opportunity to be of help too.

There is an alternative way of relating. Interdependence is a healthy combination of both dependence and independence. Interdependence balances both extremes and allows you to be self-reliant while exercising a healthy dependence on others at the same time. Imagine an emotional teeter-totter, moving comfortably together—one may be up, the other down, but both friends maintain and enjoy a steady, balanced give and take. Establishing a level of interdependence between friends begins with the choices you make. Variables like personal boundaries, limits, and honest communication can help establish a healthy sense of interdependence between friends.

Solutions

You may believe your responsibility as a Christian is to unconditionally help others, regardless of their actions, and no matter what the cost. You may think it's wrong to turn away from any friend in need, even when they make the same mistakes time and again. Christians are instructed to "love thy neighbor as thyself" (Matt. 19:19 KJV). This is truth, and it is wise to understand that you can sometimes love more when you help less.

People frequently say, "God helps those who help themselves." The same can be said for friends. It's not particularly beneficial to do for friends what they must choose to do for themselves. You also do no favors by protecting friends from experiencing the consequences of their unhealthy choices.

Enabling friends to continue destructive behaviors or coming to the rescue each time they flounder will likely find you both sinking from the weight of poor decisions. You can take steps to empower the person you care about by guiding them towards healthy decisions and positive self-care, but only your friend can be the one to take responsibility for the problem and commit herself to change. In the meantime, you can increase your own resiliency and minimize the impact of stress in your life that may be generated by the ongoing troubles of others.

Boundaries and Balance

> The wonderful thing about my best friend is that she has strong boundaries with no sharp edges. Rhoda (age 44)

A boundary on a map shows the margins of an area, and the borders surrounding it. In the same way, invisible personal boundaries that exist between people define the limits of their relationships. Parameters establish the purpose and responsibility for each friend in a relationship the way a doctor/patient, counselor/client, or teacher/student association might. Boundaries help you know the areas for which you are and are not responsible. They help maintain a healthy level of interdependence between friends.

Appropriate boundaries can effectively place limits, restricting your involvement in the unhealthy behaviors of others. When you communicate boundaries openly, with love and respect, there are no sharp edges to hurt people or wound friendships. You can be firm and kind while establishing the necessary limits in your relationships.

Boundaries indicate love and respect for your friends, but are also evidence that love and respect for yourself is a priority too. They help you balance the needs of others with the needs of your own; your needs become a vital part of the equation.

High maintenance friends tend to frequently cross boundaries, and unless told, rarely recognize when they've over-stepped their limits. Establishing consistent boundaries begins with assertive, honest communication and learning when to say no. It's crucial to develop the ability to turn down appeals for help or demands that aren't realistic or wise. This is an important first step in learning self-respect and how to to act on significant needs of your own.

Many women say it's difficult to say no to a friend. In her book, *The Book of No; 250 Ways to Say It –and Mean It and Stop People-Pleasing Forever*, Dr. Susan Newman writes, "Saying no will not turn you into a bully or make you insensitive or petty. You won't stop helping others, but you'll become more discerning about how you respond and to whom. By being more selective, you'll protect your health, have time for yourself, and assist only those you want to help whose friendships you want to preserve."

Sometimes a fine line exists between when to help and when to say no. The friends who legitimately need your help are often the women you tend to give freely to without a second thought. Friends whose circumstances give you reason to pause often need to be considered more cautiously. Situations that create feelings of doubt or anxiety may be a signal that it's not wise to intervene. Listen carefully and trust your feelings. Take your time to ponder and pray before you commit to anything asked of you.

The first sign of an unhealthy relationship often surfaces in how relaxed or tense you are around a person. You may find yourself always trying too hard to make things right. Katharine (age 46) said:

> The first place I feel it is in my stomach...a knot forms from the tension. I have a friend who is so high strung and desperate for me to hear all her problems that I feel a sense of dread when I see her coming. I resent the time she spends with me because nothing ever changes; she's always mad at the world, and she never listens to what I say anyway.

A high maintenance friend may have insatiable needs and problems into which she endlessly draws you. Sometimes a person's difficulties are due to mental health conditions characterized by patterns of repeated, negative behaviors. Some tell-tale signs or symptoms might be a low tolerance for distress or significant issues with anger. Unrelenting demands and a perspective of continuous victimization are common too. As might be expected, these individuals suffer ongoing difficulties in interpersonal relationships. A sense of urgency often accompanies the problems a person with mental health issues encounters.

Be in tune with your emotions and physical reactions, and be prepared to establish boundaries around your time with any friend who pushes your stress buttons. Saying no and setting limits will go a long way in helping you cope with a difficult friend. At the same time, be ready to direct her to helpful resources. For example, you might refer her to local counseling agencies, her pastor, or if necessary, crisis intervention resources for immediate and appropriate support.

Setting Limits

Some women admit to feeling they must rescue others. Joni (age 40) said:

> I have always come to everyone's emotional rescue. I feel guilty if I don't help, even when I don't have time. I just keep on helping, sometimes even at the expense of my husband and kids. I think I learned it from my mom who taught me it was important to try and make everyone happy. I'm exhausted and stressed out! But people expect it of me, and assume I'll drop everything for them, and so I do. I drop everything just to keep them happy.

Joni's welcome mat has turned her into a doormat. The anxiety and stress this dynamic creates is formidable. Joni's friendships are clearly out of balance, and she has come to believe that her value rests on her ability to please others. This is a dangerous habit to continue, jeopardizing her most important relationships with her family, and even her relationship with herself.

To help a friend or acquaintance with high needs requires an understanding of how you can love someone and safeguard yourself at the same time. Setting limits is a way to communicate healthy boundaries and practice good self-care. Learn to set limits from the start. Each day make intentional, conscious choices about how much time you give and how you will respond to a friend in need.

What you can do:

- Pay attention to the level of stress you have when spending time with friends. Generally the more stress you feel, the more boundaries you'll need to establish.
- Maintain balance in your life. Evaluate every request a friend makes against your own needs and schedule, as well as the priorities of loved ones.
- Learn to say, "No. I can't help you, but here's another idea or resource that might help."

• Refuse to be manipulated by anger if it's directed at you. Don't let someone else's rage or resentment control actions or decisions that are good for you.

• When overwhelmed by a friend's situation or demands, remind yourself: "It's not my responsibility or mine to fix." Step back or step out of the situation completely.

• Imagine the worst case scenario with a high maintenance friend in your life. Build healthy habits by practicing what you will say and do. For example, "I'm sorry you're upset and having a hard night, but this isn't a good time to call me or for you to come over. Thanks for understanding."

• Consider the limits you can put in place to help prevent the worst case scenario from occurring: "I don't take calls after 9:00 p.m., and I limit my conversations on the phone during the day. I'll only be able to talk at times we've agreed upon ahead of time. I appreciate your understanding."

• Decide what you will and will not do for a friend:

– I will respond to requests that I'm completely comfortable with. I won't respond to demands that are unhealthy for me.

– I will offer a ride to the bus; I won't drive all the way across town.

– I will listen to problems; I won't try to fix them.

– I'll see her when it's a good day for me; I won't change my plans at the drop of a hat.

• Communicate your limits up front. Say exactly what you can and cannot do. Practice clear and direct responses:

– I won't bail you out of this, but I will be here to listen.

– I'm willing to help you look at the pro's and con's of this situation, but the decision is yours to make.

– I don't have the solutions for you, but I'm willing to brainstorm ideas together.

– I'd like to help and be a good friend to you, but I can't

be available to you at all times, or in the way you'd like.

– I would like to help you find more support. I'll e-mail you some contacts that might be helpful.

– My family needs must come first; I'm not able to take time away from them to see you today.

- It's necessary to set clear limits for someone who has trouble accepting your time constraints. For example:

– I have 10 minutes to sit with you before I need to leave.

– Please call me before you drop by so I can let you know if it's a good time or not.

– I can only get together from 1:00-2:00 on Saturday.

– I'm sorry I can't help you with this, but I hope you'll seek support from the names and numbers I've given you.

- Tell it like it is. Be honest. You don't need to justify your reasons or make excuses for the limits you set.
- Let your boundaries and limits exist free of guilt. Remember, they're important to maintaining healthy choices and positive outcomes in your life.
- If you continue to feel the need to rescue friends, consider exploring this issue with a professional counselor. A therapist may be able to assist you in finding more satisfying ways to meet your crucial priorities. A counselor can also help you find a healthy balance between giving and receiving within relationships.

Responding To a Meltdown

Some high maintenance friends repeatedly experience emotional emergencies. In a meltdown, some women may seem to unravel and fall apart right before your eyes. They may be frantic to see you in hopes you will pick up the pieces of their life that seem to continually crash down around them.

Seeing a friend in distress, even when it's self-induced, is difficult. When you feel pressure to help with someone's unrelenting life drama's or demands, the urgency of their situation and the need for attention can be overwhelming. You may feel you have no choice but to try and help. In this case, be prepared to stand firm and approach a high maintenance friend from a healthy position. Scripture supports behavior that doesn't enable or rescue others and demonstrates love at the same time. "if you rescue . . . you will have to do it again" (Proverbs 19:19). It's important to allow people to bear the natural consequences of their actions so they have the opportunity to learn and grow. Consider the following suggestions for ways to accomplish this.

What you can do:

• Talk less and listen more. Focus on seeing the problem from your friend's point of view. This will help diffuse anger and frustration.

• Validate all thoughts and feelings: "I understand." "I agree." "Good point; tell me more." "I see why you feel the way you do."

• Demonstrate empathy: "This must be a painful experience for you to have to go through." "This is a really tough situation for you to be in." Empathy is more helpful than giving advice. Advice from others is often not followed or wanted in situations where unhealthy choices are being made or when people are reticent to take control of situations that are hurtful. Make it a rule not to give advice unless asked.

• Direct intervention and forthright counsel may be clearly warranted in situations where safety is a concern. However, don't necessarily expect your recommendations to be followed, no matter how sound or logical they might be. (See "When a Friend is Struggling with Mental Health Issues" for mental health emergencies.)

• Explore with a troubled friend what choices contributed to her distress and how she might take responsibility for her actions beginning today.

• Don't make assumptions about someone's circumstances or behaviors. Things are not always what they seem. A situation that sounds like a catastrophe today may be nearly forgotten tomorrow. Women who demonstrate moods that shift from one extreme to another may not be seeing circumstances clearly or interpreting the reactions of others accurately either.

• If a friend lashes out at you in anger, refuse to jump in the ring with her. Instead, listen and kindly withdraw. Take care of yourself, and when she's calm again, express how you felt under her attack. For example, "When you scream at me, I feel demeaned and unable to stay and talk with you."

• Encourage your friend to focus on what she can do to solve the problem: "What needs to happen for this to change, or for you to get past this?" "What can you do today to help yourself feel better?"

• Continue to bring your conversation back to a place of encouragement and hopefulness: "I know you have strengths and abilities to overcome this." "You deserve to take good care of yourself. You are worth it."

• Encourage your friend to breathe, relax, and clear her mind regularly as she speaks.

• Follow through with what you say. Leave when it's time for you to leave, and don't make promises you can't keep. You can say, "I have to go now, but I will pray for you and check in with you tomorrow."

Dangerous Friendships: Sex, Drugs, and Drama Queens

Be mindful; your friendship choices can help you grow closer to God or cause you to distance from Him. Maintaining boundaries and saying no will help. So will setting limits when necessary. But sometimes women find themselves in situations they hadn't anticipated. Scripture supports the need to protect yourself and to "guard your heart" from sinful behavior as well as from the immaturity of others. Unhealthy situations can be avoided or more effectively handled when you're prepared ahead of time to remain true to your values and beliefs.

Sex

Patricia (age 31) talks about a close friend of the same age who started having an extra-marital affair:

> A friend of mine was having multiple affairs and telling me all the sordid details every time we got together. Even as our husbands chatted innocently in the next room . . . and our children played together outside! The way she laughed and snickered about it made me feel sick inside. I felt guilty carrying her secret, and disloyal, as if I had just participated in the act myself! I stopped contacting her when I saw how unhealthy it was for me . . . I felt guilty by association. I tried to be a friend. I tried to understand her vulnerability and obsession with other men. I suggested she see a therapist, but I don't think she ever considered it. I finally couldn't be around her any longer. I had to avoid all contact. I never condoned her behavior, ever . . . but I do wonder if there's more I could've done.

In some cases a friend might listen to a trusted person's opinions and feelings, and be persuaded to make a different choice. Other times, a person is set on continuing destructive behavior regardless of the suggestions and guidance others offer. Katharine went on to say, "It killed me inside. I wanted to scream at her for betraying her family, risking her health, and her husband's health ... it was WRONG! Looking back, I wish I had told her the truth about how I felt. Instead, I kept quiet and tried to change the subject."

When trust and respect are present between friends, it's important to bolster your courage and be honest. Express how a friend's unhealthy choices and behaviors have affected you. Opening up about how you feel may raise accountability and shake a friend from the illusion that what she is doing isn't harmful to herself and others. It's okay to tell her you won't continue to listen to what you can't morally condone. It's right to risk being truthful, especially when you care about one another. More importantly, remaining someone's confidant when bad choices continue validate poor choices and isn't healthy for you.

Mia (age 39) said:

> To be honest, after hearing about the affair my married friend was having, I began to entertain the idea myself. It just stirred up such intense longings for that kind of passion and romance again. I have no reason to even want to be with another man. I really don't. But it did plant that seed in my mind, and so I had to dig it out and keep my thinking straight. I spiced things up again with my husband, and it reminded me that everything I could ever want, I already have.

As I Corinthians 15:33-34 (NIV) reminds us, "Do not be

misled: 'Bad company corrupts good character.'" Not all friends who make mistakes, even tragic ones, are "bad company." However, those who continue on a deliberate path of sinful choices are those who can corrupt. Unhealthy choices can often seem like attractive, viable options for anyone. They're subtly inducing, so women are wise to hold on to their moral compass and keep their bearings. True friends support one another in doing just that. They back upright decisions, rather than seek agreement to justify wrong decisions.

Sexual sin is easily available on the Internet and everywhere in the media. Within American society, it's become a destructive force in many people's lives. Pornography and sexual addiction are not just problems for men or teens. In today's culture, women are participating in increasing numbers. The constant barrage of detrimental messages about sex communicate less about love and commitment and more about instant self-gratification and seductive looks. Both men and women are experiencing the effects of another cultural shift in attitudes about sexual behaviors. In the 60s the slogan was, "If it feels good, do it!" Today, the harmful cliché might be, "Anything goes."

Karen shared this experience:

> I met Renee in the hospital. We both had surgery for ovarian cysts and sympathized with each other's aches and pains. We became good friends and helped each other laugh away the hours spent in our hospital room. Of course it was the most painful thing in the world so we had to hold pillows over our bellys to support our fits of laughter. Our friendship continued, and we used to meet for lunch or coffee and chat away for hours. We laughed a lot, just like in the hospital, and I had so much fun with her! Then one

> day at lunch, while sipping my wonton soup, she said to me, "You know, my boyfriend would be mad if I saw another guy, but he doesn't care if I'm with a girl. I was just wondering if you'd be interested in a threesome." I instantly choked and spit out my soup. She made it clear I was too "uptight" and needed to experience different things. She was right. I needed to experience a different friendship. Sadly, this one wasn't going to work.

Women don't have to see eye-to-eye on everything. Chapter two demonstrates the opportunities that abound in differences between friends. However, when behaviors threaten your sense of self, safety, morality, or compromise your spiritual beliefs, it's safe to say they are not healthy decisions. Sometimes you have to just say no and make an immediate exit.

Marni (age 46) shared a different challenge around sex and women's views of it. She said this:

> It's awkward to be with a friend, or a group of women, when they start talking about male celebrities in a worshipful, "Isn't he the sexiest?" way. I don't like it when they treat men as sex objects any more than I like it when men do that to women!

Doreen (age 32) agrees. As a professor at a large college, she sees the evidence of a double standard all the time. In her experience, women of faith and non-believers alike have adopted a more casual outlook about their sexuality and have embraced the very views feminists have fought so long and hard against. She said:

> Don't get me wrong, I'm all for sex; I love it with my husband, but to be at an all female party with a male

> stripper is my idea of hell. I just don't get it, and some of my women friends who see it as innocent fun don't understand that.

It's a challenge to be like a salmon swimming upstream against the current. The world is full of healthy and unhealthy messages about sexuality. Where you draw the line and refuse to participate is up to you, but God gives clear guidelines. Being true to yourself means upholding your values and respecting your own ideas, even without the support of your friends. Proverbs 4:14-15 says this: "Do not walk in the way of evil. Avoid it, do not travel on it; turn away from it and pass on" (NKJV).

Drugs

Some women will do anything for a friend. Marsha (age 30) admits she was so anxious to have a friend in her life that she compromised her own good judgment. Her choices landed her in court and in jail for a shoplifting conviction. Marsha knew her friend had stolen some prescription drugs, and she knew her friend's money was going to illegal drugs. Still, when her friend pressured her to shoplift, she struggled with how to say no and didn't choose to walk away. Instead, Marsha was arrested when her friend dropped several items in her bag before she walked out the door. She literally was left "holding the bag." Marsha said this:

> I didn't want to do this for my friend, but I didn't want her to be mad at me either! She was my only friend at the time. I tried to tell her no, but she kept pleading with me, telling me it would be okay and begged me to help her. She said if I could help just this once, she would never ask me again. So she dropped this stuff in my bag, and I didn't know what

to do! She left the store, and I chased after her trying to tell her "No! I can't do this!" But it was too late. As soon as I put one foot out the door, security guards stopped me. And my friend left me to the wolves, and never once even apologized. Now I ask myself, "Why didn't I stand up to her?"

The old saying is true: "With friends like that, who needs enemies?" They will leave you in the lurch every time. Marsha learned the hard way. She realized she had been used and needed to reassess her own values. Today she is learning how to discern trustworthy friends from those who are self-centered and driven by unhealthy choices. She said:

> So now I have radar, an antenna my counselor has helped me tune into. I pick up on signals now, sometimes subtle ones, like self-absorption and demanding expectations. And I've learned to look at whether behaviors are healthy ones or not. If friends need to steal, use drugs or alcohol, then I know being a good friend to me isn't high on their list.

Drama Queens

> It's hard to be with friends who need to be in the spotlight all the time, especially the kind that have to have everyone's attention. They are either self-centered or used to monopolizing conversation, or they thrive on gossip and embellish everything they hear. Everyone around a drama queen becomes part of her audience. It's not a relationship; it's a performance. *—Margie (age 40)*

Sharing gossip and relaying stories about other people are unhealthy choices that nearly everyone can make.

Proverbs 16:28 (NKJV) reminds us: "A perverse man sows strife, and a whisperer separates the best of friends."

Women say the drama queens in their lives don't necessarily "whisper." Their message is usually delivered loud and clear to anyone who will listen. Regardless, gossip hurts! Not only friendships, but real people can be damaged or destroyed in the process. Drama queens are tough to be around. It can be a challenge to rein them in and personally destructive if they aren't avoided.

Dangerous friendships involving sex, drugs, or drama queens require courageous actions, stamina, and wisdom. You can learn to respond with confidence and peace when faced with the hard choices and situations any of these friendship challenges bring.

What you can do:

- Swim upstream when you need to; part of living your own life means going against the grain, just like Jesus did.
- Commit to making healthy choices, even when everyone else around you isn't.
- Trust your feelings. Expect the Holy Spirit to guide your life with emotional responses and first impressions. Ask for discernment regarding people.
- Don't be a victim. Think for yourself and live your own life.
- If you feel insignificant among your current friends, spend time with friends who know you are valuable.
- Set your own goals not those that might please others.
- Support and encourage all the healthy choices you see your friends make.
- Walk away when someone uses the spotlight to gossip about others.
- Recognize when someone is manipulating you. Like

Marsha, learn to trust your instincts when you feel pressured or bribed to do something you have doubts about, or when dishonest tactics in any form are being suggested.

• Refuse to listen or participate in gossip, deceit, and choices you know are wrong. Make the decision to be different. Make courageous decisions, and then commit to follow through with them.

• Remember Proverbs 12:18: "The tongue of the wise promotes health" (NKJV). Be wise; personal peace will be your reward.

When a Friend Is Being Abused

> One of the biggest challenges for me is seeing friends who are talented, compassionate, smart, and loving endure an abusive relationship. Sometimes it's hard to know how to be their friend. *—Liza (age 51)*

Since the beginning of time, people have resorted to violence as a means of taking control, revenge, and gaining power over others. Violence at the hands of those you love isn't anything new either. Christians suffer abuse in their homes as frequently as any other sector in society.

Domestic violence is a pattern of physical, sexual, emotional, spiritual and/or economic abuse. It crosses all class, cultural, racial and religious boundaries. An abuser may hit, slap, shove, or choke. He may hurt his partner's feelings by name calling or making fun of her. He may also force her into sex or doing sexual things she doesn't want to do. Clearly, not all victims are female. Men are also battered and suffer equally devastating effects of abuse. However, since the majority of women are battered by men in domestic violence situations—and this book is about women—the offender will be referred to in the male gender throughout this chapter.

Domestic violence happens as a means to take power and control over someone. In 1979 Lenore Walker wrote a classic book, *The Battered Woman,* in which she identified a cycle of abuse. This continuous cycle is characterized by escalating tension, violence, remorse, and the victim's belief it will never happen again. In the honeymoon, or remorse stage, manipulation of a victim can be subtle, often showing up in the form of apologies, sincere regret, and promises to get help.

God has a tender heart toward those who have been victimized by cruelty and violence. Whether these attacks are physical, verbal, sexual, or spiritual, women need to do what they can to remove themselves from abusive and potentially violent relationships. However, most victims of domestic violence hesitate to involve law enforcement and the legal system in their lives—even when their lives depend on it. Deborah (age 50) explained why she was reluctant to report to the police:

> When my husband pinned me against the wall and threatened to kill me, I knew I had to do something. But when I watched the police take him away, it was one of the hardest things I've ever had to do. If he had been an unknown intruder, I could have witnessed the arrest with relief and satisfaction! But this was the man I loved and chose to marry. I still loved him and he said he still loved me! It was painful and agonizing, and I felt sorry for him. I knew he needed me. But ultimately I learned that love wasn't enough to prevent his explosive rages or intent to harm me. I had to protect myself and he needed to experience the consequences of his behavior. Now when I look back on that day, I realize it

was not only the right thing to do, it's what God directed me to do.

The choice to take the abuser back is another judgment call that is often made on an emotional, rather than rational level. Linda (age 30) had this experience:

> After the police intervened, he called me from jail and thanked me. He told me I was right to have him arrested and that he was afraid of himself too. He apologized and took full responsibility. He said he'd go to treatment, and promised me this would never happen again. I loved him; I missed him, and I felt I owed him and our relationship another chance.
>
> My counselor predicted that within 4-6 months another incident would likely occur; only this time, it would be worse. She created a safety plan with me. She warned me that the rage would only grow stronger. And she was right. His words told me "thank you, I deserved to go to jail," but when his jealousy and possessiveness of me were triggered, he snapped again. This time it was worse. His resentment of my past choices had only grown stronger, but I didn't know it until it was too late. One broken arm and three cracked ribs later, and with the help of an agency serving victims of domestic violence, I finally left him for good. Today, I'm free. I'm with a man who respects me in all ways and lives a healthy lifestyle. He has the level of mental health that's necessary to be in a relationship. In short, he lives a godly life, and that's the key.

Many men don't abuse, but it can be extremely difficult to tell which ones will. A few of the characteristics of those who might become dangerous include: men who have violent families, those who get angry over small things, and those who are in the habit of blaming others for their problems. Other indicators include jealousy and low self-esteem. Some mistreat animals and abuse drugs and alcohol. Most are overcontrolling in their behaviors and words, and try to keep the woman in their life isolated.

Violence against women has little to do with an offender's stress and anger problems. It doesn't happen because he loses his temper in a moment of anger, or drank too much alcohol and didn't know what he was doing. Those who abuse women and children are often driven to do so because of significant character flaws and psychopathology. Their behavior stems from core wounds within that take concerted effort and time to be healed and corrected. It's a long road that takes most men years to finish if they are able to stay the course with the counsel of a professional.

When the abuser is as lethal and dangerous as Linda's offender, it's never safe for the abused woman to go back. However, many women choose to do just that.

Lynn (age 54) formerly a victim of abuse, helped a friend who was threatened and physically restrained by her boyfriend. Based on her own experience, Lynn cautioned her friend about returning to the relationship even though the offender was reportedly making all the changes requested of him. She offered this perspective:

> By telling your boyfriend what he needs to do in order for you to see him again, you've essentially given him instructions on how to get you back. He'll be motivated to do the work, but now it's for you, not for him. That never works because once he has you back, the old behavior will return. You'll never be free of this cycle of abuse if you don't end the rela-

> tionship completely. I don't think this is important just for you, but for your boyfriend too! I realize you still care about him; I had those feelings too, but all the promises in the world can't alter the unhealthy dynamic between the two of you. If you leave him and he gets help, he may have the chance to do better with someone else in the future. I know this isn't what you wanted to hear. And I know the right thing is always the hardest to do.

Some women tolerate abuse and disrespect because they don't feel worthy of healthy relationships. Gloria, age 54 made this observation about other women caught in the cycle of abuse:

> The smartest women act dumb when it comes to men. They get involved and repeat the cycle with abusive, disturbed men. Love is blind. She thinks she can change him, but most often she will change for him. It makes me want to scream!

Women cannot change an offender's abuse, and they cannot stop violence by changing their own behavior. The abuser needs expert help in learning how to stop controlling others when under stress and stop using violence as a response to underlying wounds.

Women can learn protection strategies. After extracting herself from an abusive marriage, Jacqui (age 52) said:

> Believe me, it would only take the slightest encouragement, and my ex-husband would be right back with me. I've always had trouble explaining to people why I don't even speak to him. Most people assume it's out of anger or hatred. It's not. It's self-preservation. I won't make myself available to his manipula-

tion and games ever again. I had to permanently cut off all contact in order to protect myself.

Living in an abusive relationship is exhausting and stressful. Abused women need supportive friends with whom they can talk openly and discuss plans and options. Countless women say if it hadn't been for an honest, steadfast friend, they would've never mustered the strength and courage to press charges against an abusive partner. The best way to support an abused friend through the trauma and sadness of domestic violence is to consider the following guidance and recommendations.

What you can do:

- Tell her 100% of the responsibility for violence rests with the offender. Let her know she didn't cause him to act the way he did no matter what she did. It's never the abused woman's fault.
- Remind her that abuse is not caused by alcohol or drug abuse or a short temper. The problems go much deeper, and the solutions do too.
- Care enough to get involved. Ask directly if she is being hurt in any way in her relationship.
- Listen whenever she can talk about the abuse. Acknowledge the seriousness and validate her feelings.
- Take risks to intervene safely on behalf of anyone being threatened or abused. Call the police immediately if you witness an assault or think you hear domestic violence occurring anywhere.
- Help your friend understand she is worthy, and has the right to take responsibility for her own protection. Offer to help protect her from the abuse. Direct her to a safe place, and help her find the support services she needs through a local organization assisting victims of domestic violence.

(See "Helplines" for national organizations at the end of this book.)

• Don't judge your friend! Don't criticize her actions, feelings, or decisions even when you disagree and are frightened by the danger she's experiencing. By trying to control her actions and decisions, you are repeating the same dynamics as her abuser. You can help more by saying, "I'm afraid for your safety. It's likely to get worse, so know I'm here for you whenever you're ready to leave." Respect and love will serve her more effectively.

• If a friend is unwilling to leave the abusive relationship, encourage her to develop a safety plan with the help of a domestic violence agency or counselor. An appropriate safety plan includes all the steps a victim will take when the next incident of violence or abuse occurs and includes a list of important documents to take with her if and when she decides to leave. (See "Helplines" for further resources.)

• You can also tell your friend:
  - You have the right to be safe, and so do your children and pets.
  - You do not deserve to be hurt or threatened.
  - You have the right not to be put down, made fun of, or embarrassed.
  - You have the right to go wherever and see whomever you choose.
  - You have the right to express your opinions and have them respected.
  - You have the right to have your needs be as important as your partner's.
  - You have the right to grow and change in your own way.
  - You have the right to break up and fall out of love and not be threatened.

• Help her avoid isolation. Remind her she is not alone.

Encourage her to attend a support group at least twice.

• Remind her of the kind of care and treatment she deserves by giving her a spa experience such as a pedicure, massage, or facial. Better yet, go along and enjoy being pampered together.

• Don't minimize verbal cruelty; it's just as painful and harmful as a physical assault. Help your friend understand being teased, criticized, called names, or put down, are all forms of verbal abuse that undermine her sense of self. This form of abuse is also a means to control her.

• Help her realize she deserves a mutually respectful relationship; one in which she is not controlled or bossed around, does not hide her views or values, and can freely express different opinions.

• Be aware that spiritual abuse takes many forms. Being led to believe you are unworthy of God's love and grace are common tactics abusers use, especially those with rigid, fear-based religious doctrines.

• Share the support and courage God gives in times of trouble. Help her recognize He sees all forms of abuse as unacceptable. Scripture clearly supports a woman's choice to leave, protect herself, call the police, and press charges.

• Don't pressure, suggest, or expect her to immediately forgive the offender. Instead, remind her that it's a process that takes time.

• Share scripture that will serve to comfort and strengthen her. See Soul Solutions at the end of this chapter.

• Be honest and direct about your feelings, but make it clear you will love and support your friend regardless of her decision to stay or leave. Maintaining your relationship is crucial if she is to safely extricate herself from harm in the future. Unfortunately, she will need you even more the next time around.

When a Friend Is Struggling With Addiction

Webster's Encylopedic Dictionary describes addiction as the "state of being enslaved to a habit or practice or to something that is psychologically or physically habit-forming, to such an extent that its cessation causes severe trauma." Addiction can happen by becoming dependent on substances like alcohol and drugs, or by becoming dependent on chemical-producing behaviors such as immoral sex, overeating, excessive spending, gambling, or dangerous thrill-seeking. Whichever form it takes, addiction is an attempt to fill a void in one's life.

Usually those who suffer from an addiction have had significant experiences of unmet needs for love, attention, and nurturing. Using substances or engaging in compulsive behaviors are attempts to self-medicate pain and loneliness. These individuals are often angry and don't know what real love is. Most were denied healthy attachments as children. Personal wounds or hurts that stem from trauma and abuse are important for substance abusers to face in professional counseling.

Some women spend a lifetime avoiding feelings, preferring to stay numb. Under the influence of their addiction, they maintain the illusion they're in control. Over time the consequences of self-destructive behavior eventually show the irony of the belief that they can control their lives better than God.

If you have a friend struggling with an addiction, be prepared for denial and possible defensiveness. When addicts aren't ready to give up their drug or behavior, they will go to great lengths to convince all around them that they can manage it without any harmful or serious consequences. But a negative spiral is inevitable.

Char's friend, a 36 year-old woman, said this:

> My drinking doesn't affect my job or relationships so it's not a problem. I've never missed a day of work, and it doesn't change me. I'm just physically able to drink a lot of alcohol and be absolutely fine. This is just who I am; and if you don't like it, I really don't care.

Char was faced with the difficult challenge of confronting her friend's denial. Every time her alcoholic friend drove while drinking, crashed her car, or got in an argument, it tested the bounds of their friendship. Char learned to speak assertively and make different choices when she spent time with her. She refused to drive with her, took her keys when she needed to, and would not bail her out of problems that were a result of drinking. Eventually, Char had to set even tougher limits. She told her that until she was clean and sober, she was unable to be around her. Char offered this woman complete support when, two years later, she entered treatment for alcohol dependency.

You cannot fix a friend's addiction problems or save her from ruin. And it's wise not to try. You can best show your love for a friend by refusing to enable her addiction or perpetuate her denial. Remain non-judgmental and recognize she needs to make the decision to stop.

Women from every profession, culture, and age group experience addiction. They attend church, college, raise families, and hold down jobs. Today younger women are more prone to alcohol abuse while addiction to prescription drugs is more common among women of all ages. Lucy, a professional businesswoman, was addicted to prescription pain killers at the age of 40.

> My best friend told me I had a problem before I even realized it. She is the one who pointed me in the

> right direction and helped get me to the point where I would seek help. She didn't mince words. Just told me straight out what I needed to do, and then backed away until I followed through.

Addiction does not get better, improve over time or go away. It cannot be managed, controlled, or cut back. These are dangerous myths. A good friend educates herself, and makes the choice not to buy into statements of denial. Al Anon and Nar-Anon groups provide the education and advice you need to learn how to support friends through the ups and downs of the recovery process. (Contact information for these groups are listed in Helplines at the end of the book.) Keep in mind the following when helping a friend.

What you can do:

• Don't ignore addiction of any kind. Talk about it in an open and direct way, without lectures and judgmental accusations. Be honest about your observations and concerns, but remember, her addiction is not yours to fix.

• Al Anon and Nar-Anon are tremendously helpful support groups for families and friends of alcoholics or substance abusers. Consider attending a group for family and friends to learn more about how you can best help her as well as find support for yourself.

• Refuse to make excuses for a friend's addiction. Don't minimize it, justify it, or help her hide it. Don't collude with the addiction, or you'll become part of the problem.

• As tempting as it can be, refrain from rescuing a friend from the consequences of unhealthy behavior. Those who are addicted often need to experience the full impact of their problem before they are willing to get help. There is a bottom line they often have to hit.

• Be firm and consistent about your values, limits, and

level of support. Unacceptable choices and behaviors don't have to be tolerated.

• Getting well requires her to admit powerlessness over the addiction and acceptance of the need for professional help.

• Ongoing support groups like Alcoholics Anonymous (AA) can provide regular accountability. They serve to remind and encourage the steps that must be taken for lasting recovery.

• Be prepared for relapses. Freedom from addiction can't happen overnight, and for most, recovery is a long and challenging process. Many addicted people go back to using their drug of choice a number of times before recovery sticks. This can be frustrating and frightening for those who love them.

• Remaining calm and patient will accomplish more than giving ultimatums, blaming, or giving up on her when she hasn't been able to stay clean or sober. Continue a firm but loving stance in the face of success as well as failures.

• Understand medical assessments and intervention may be necessary. Appropriate medications may need to be prescribed as well.

• Keep in mind treatment for addiction almost always requires specialized programs and help from experienced professionals trained in the field of addiction. Staying clean, sober, and changing destructive behaviors requires participation in ongoing emotional, spiritual, physical, and psychological work.

When a Friend Is Struggling With Mental Health Issues

Good mental health leads to a positive self-image and satisfying relationships with friends and others. It fosters correct decisions, helping you deal effectively with life's challenges. Mental stability inspires positive thoughts, feelings, and behaviors. It's as important as physical health; in fact, the two are closely linked, each affecting the other. Mental health deserves the same attention and care as any physical ailment or disease.

Depression is one of the most common mental health challenges women face today. Other mood disorders are prevalent too, along with anxiety, post-traumatic stress, and eating disorders. None of these challenges is a result of personal weakness, lack of character, spiritual immaturity, or a matter of will power. The emotional discomfort and pain people experience is real. Often there are chemical imbalances in the brain as well as life circumstances that contribute to the development of serious problems. It's also believed that people have a genetic predisposition to depression, anxiety, and other mental health conditions in the same way they may be predisposed to heart disease or diabetes.

Coping with any form of mental health challenge is difficult. It is often perceived as a character weakness, so the symptoms that impact the heart, mind, body, and soul may therefore go untreated. Women may feel alone and often say they feel crazy, different, and afraid.

Helping a friend seek professional assistance is important, and so is standing by her as she works through the challenges she must face. Women need to be assured they are not crazy. Often what has happened to them is crazy. Life can be full of all kinds of unusual and confusing experiences, but remind her she has good reasons for her reactions and symptoms. Mental health issues are part of the human condition, and most people will experience this first-hand at some point in their lives. People long to know they are not the only one who has ever known the sometimes bizarre experiences that accompany a mental illness. Normalize your friend's reactions and offer hope and reassurance. Though you can't fix this problem for her, she needs to know she's not alone, and that reliable treatment is available.

What you can do:

- If a friend has attempted suicide or has made a plan to harm herself or someone else, make an emergency 9-1-1 call or immediately escort her to the nearest hospital emergency room.
- Don't be afraid to ask directly if she has thoughts of suicide or harming others. Contrary to what some people think, asking about suicidal thoughts won't plant the idea in her mind. However, not asking may lead to an even greater crisis.
- Remain respectful. Calmly express your confidence in her ability to get through any crisis and remind her, "It won't always feel as bad as it does right now."
- Stand by your friend. She is not crazy. She is reacting to a very real physical imbalance, traumatic life event, or circumstance that has overwhelmed her.
- Remember, given enough stress or wrong circumstances, everyone will show distressing mental health reactions in some form.
- Be open and supportive to the use of psychotherapy and medication as recommended for her safety and well-being. Treatment is usually more successful when therapy and medication are combined.
- Add your spiritual support to her recovery through prayer; continually share God's words of comfort and healing.
- Educate yourself about your friend's diagnosis and the issues she is confronting. Understand the challenges she

must face every day in order to offer the best support you can.

• Learn to recognize the symptoms of serious depression and eating disorders. See the "Behavior Checklist" under "When to Seek Further Help" sections.

• Learn to speak openly about symptoms, behaviors, and the seriousness of the problem you see. If she has not sought help, talk to her about your concerns and offer specific examples of why you are worried about her.

• Do your best to exercise love and patience at all times, realizing you may sometimes fall short. With God's help, forgive yourself and try again tomorrow!

• Believe her when she tells you how she feels. Mental health problems can give people a distorted view of reality. Don't try to talk her out of feelings, instead point out alternative ideas and perspectives. Whenever possible offer a more accurate view, based on reality and the facts. Encourage her to seek professional help if she hasn't already done so.

• Assure her she is not alone. Help her avoid isolation by offering to help her stay involved in life. Attend church at the same time, take a walk, or go out for a cup of coffee together.

• Encourage your friend to practice positive self-care, including proper nutrition, daily exercise, relaxation, and quiet time with God.

• Support positive actions and goals, but suggest simple ideas; encourage her to take one step at a time for guaranteed success.

• Celebrate every accomplishment, no matter how small the step may seem.

• Help her be accountable to you and others who can offer support through the especially difficult or dark periods during her recovery.

- Encourage her to avoid addictive behaviors and unhealthy relationships as a means of coping or escaping current problems.
- Recommend service to others. Giving feels good, and serving others has been shown to effectively help treat depression.
- Suggest she keep a Gratitude Journal. Ask her to look for and expect at least one blessing each day. Whether small or large, encourage her to pay attention to good things that come her way every day. Thankfulness for a better night's sleep, a new book to read, or waking to rays of sunshine on a cloudless day are tangible blessings.
- Remind her that recovery is a combination of helping yourself and letting others help you.
- Give hope. Even though it can sometimes be a long process, with professional help people do improve, fully recover, or learn to manage symptoms successfully.

When to Seek Further Help

While it's not unusual to feel upset, sad, angry, or confused at one time or another, these feelings become significant when they are recurrent or extreme. Suicidal or homicidal thoughts and feelings, or any unsafe behaviors that could potentially threaten health and safety, are critical to address immediately. When behaviors and symptoms of any kind are chronic, help should be sought without delay.

If a friend is in an abusive relationship, or battling addiction, it's always wise to suggest options for treatment and ongoing professional support. It can be difficult when a friend resists your help, but remember, it's better to risk losing the friendship than to lose her forever. Do whatever you can to ensure her safety and well-being.

Behavior Checklist:

- Unexplained injuries or questionable explanations of injuries
- Withdrawal or isolation
- Fear or nervousness
- Tearfulness
- Comments related to a partner's jealousy, possessiveness, demands, put downs
- Feeling worthless or guilty
- Finding little or no pleasure in life
- Thoughts or comments of self-harm or harm to others. (Thoughts of suicide may be overtly spoken, or communicated through subtle hints or actions such as giving things away.)
- Sudden change in mood, either happy or sad
- Fear that prevents normal daily activities
- Loss of pleasure in previously enjoyed activities
- Chronic sadness
- Sense of hopelessness about the future
- Inability to sleep or sleeping too much
- Changes in appetite, mood, sex drive, sleep patterns
- Anxiety or panic attacks
- Chronic illness and medical conditions
- Nightmares
- Irritability
- Withdrawal
- Anger
- Unusual eating habits
- Obsession with weight or distorted body image
- Secretiveness about eating
- Compulsive exercising and dieting
- Impulsive spending or shoplifting
- Experiencing racing thoughts or agitation

- Extreme or unexplained mood swings
- Losing contact with reality: hearing voices or seeing things others do not
- Believing that others are plotting against you
- Inability to communicate clearly

Soul Solutions

Healthy choices begin with a healthy relationship with God. Isaiah 58:9 provides a constant and comforting reminder, "Then you will call and the Lord will answer; You will cry and He will say, 'Here I am.'" He is a sovereign foundation and the ultimate guide for wisdom, discernment, comfort, and healing.

Negative friendships and circumstances, domestic violence, addiction, and mental health challenges all have the power to turn people away from God or draw them closer to Him. Such trials also enlarge a person's capacity to receive from God, and to invest in a meaningful relationship with Him. Through Jesus all things are possible. Psalm 68:28 affirms, "Your God has commanded your strength; show yourself strong."

Godly men and women are called to recognize the pervasiveness and harsh reality of abuse, to respond compassionately to those who suffer, and to aid in their recovery through practical and spiritual support. (See Isaiah 58:6-7; Romans 12:15; Ecclesiastes 4:1.) God's Word confirms wise guidance, and the right strategies and approaches to take in every situation that women face in life. He will support you as you learn to choose friends wisely and respond to unhealthy situations with courage and integrity. He will help you adjust and fully provide for you as you face any challenge or choice that confronts you. He promises to "equip you in every good thing to do His will" (Hebrews 13:21).

In the midst of problems, it may be hard to recognize how you can understand the purpose of difficult trials you or friends are enduring. But clearly, God's good purposes will unfold for those who allow Him to bring them through the fires of life. This can be hard to accept, but in time you will see these words from James ring true: "Consider it all joy, my brethren, when you encounter various trials; knowing that the testing of your faith produces endurance, and let endurance have its perfect result" (James 1:2-4).

In Matthew 14:22-31, Jesus commands Peter to step out on the water amid a powerful and frightening storm. Peter had to make the choice to take the first step; he had to trust it was possible. Though he had faith in Jesus, he still felt unable. He became frightened and started to sink. Jesus, who fully understands human nature, took hold of him to keep him from drowning, but still challenged him to become a man of courage and conviction. God asks no less of you or your friends. He promises to be with you when you suffer. He will never abandon you.

God can help you stand by friends when they choose to responsibly work through trials and problems. He desires you to grow from every experience that comes your way, and desires the same for your friends. Trust Him to help you make the healthy choices necessary for your ongoing emotional, physical, psychological, and spiritual growth.

Prayer Guide

Rest quietly for a few minutes, and seek God and His faithful presence to help you wash away any fear, frustration, confusion, or uncertainty. Receive of Him and know He wants to assist you, transform unhealthy choices and behaviors, and is there for you at all times, in all situations, no matter how hard. What are the current sources of your greatest concern?

Perhaps they are fear, embarrassment, shame, or confusion. Once your greatest anxieties or concerns are clear, seek God's peace, guidance, and confirmation. Then close your eyes and begin to express gratitude for His everlasting, unconditional love for you and your friends. Ask to be given the tools, strategies, and characteristics needed to handle each and every circumstance successfully. Pray to be inspired and reminded that He is always in control.

What you can do:

- God supports self care. Treat your heart, mind, body, and soul with respect and attention. Learn to set limits and boundaries to protect yourself in the face of a friend's unhealthy behavior or needs.
- Recognize all addictions are fueled by a loss of significance, peace, and love. If you can, respectfully help your friend understand there is a sense of purpose and meaning in life that only God can fill. Nothing else can serve as a substitute.
- Help your friend see her worth to God and His desire to comfort and bring her closer to Him. Through your life and example, show her the real and personal relationship with God that's possible.
- Offer to be a prayer partner, to spend time in intercessory prayer to support your friend's recovery in whatever she faces.
- Be patient; trust God's timing and the circumstances that develop. Believe He has heard, and in His own time, He will answer.
- Be respectful and patient of wherever your friend is in her own relationship with God, and in her healing from traumatic circumstances or unhealthy choices. If she's a non-believer, don't impose your beliefs on her; rather demonstrate them through your clarity of action and friendship.

Closing Scripture

Each week consider one verse you want to put into action and attitude. Take note of how these critical qualities make a difference in your relationships.

God has given each of you some special abilities; be sure to use them to help each other (1 Peter 4:10 LB).

A time to break down, and a time to build up; a time to weep, and a time to laugh (Eccl. 3:3-4 NKJV).

Let us therefore come boldly to the throne of grace, that we may obtain mercy and find grace to help in time of need (Hebrews 4:16 NKJV).

She opens her mouth in wisdom, and the teaching of kindness is on her tongue (Proverbs 31:26).

Husbands, love your wives, and do not be harsh with them (Col. 3:19 RSV).

The Lord examines both the righteous and the wicked. He hates those who love violence (Psalm 11:5 NLT).

Warn those who are unruly, comfort the faint-hearted, uphold the weak, be patient with all (1 Thessalonians 5:14 NKJV).

Do you not know that you are God's temple and that God's Spirit dwells in you? If any one destroys God's temple, God will destroy him. For God's temple is holy, and that temple you are (1 Corinthians 3:16-17 RSV).

A prudent man foresees evil and hides himself (Proverbs 27:12 NKJV).

Confess your sins to one another, and pray for one another so that you may be healed (James 5:16).

Further scriptures for victims of domestic violence:*

God's plan is that the home should be free of oppression. See Isaiah 54:5-14; Romans 12:18.

Physical violence and verbal abuse are forbidden by God. See Psalm 56:5-6; Isaiah 58:4-6; Matthew 5:22; 1 Thessalonians 4:3-6.

Silence, secrecy, or concealment are not God's ways of dealing with problems. See Matthew 10:26; Mark 4:22; Luke 8:17; 12:2-3; Ephesians 5:13-14; James 5:16.

Changed attitude and behavior rather than tears, extravagant gifts, or desperate promises bespeak genuine repentance. See Matthew 3:8; Luke 3:8; Acts 26:20; Hebrews 12:17.

Sometimes separation is the best course for the safety and peace of family members. See Genesis 13:7-11, 14:8-16, 21:9-21, 25:8-9, 27:41-45, 32:1-33, 45:4-15; Proverbs 24:1-2; Acts 16:36-40; Colossians 4:10; Philemon 24; 1 Corinthians 7:5.
A wife is an equal heir of the grace of life and not the possession of her husband. See 1 Peter 3:7; Corinthians 6:19-20.

(Special thanks to the World Evangelical Fellowship: Commission on Women's Concerns who printed a brochure with*

this information titled, "Task Force to Stop Abuse Against Women.")

Friend-to-Friend Activities

1. Self-Care Reflection

Make two lists.

First, write down the names of friends with whom you experience healthy interdependent relationships—those you experience equal give and take and mutual support.

Second, list friends with whom you've encountered difficulties—those with high needs, drama queens; friends making unhealthy choices of addictions or abuse, or those with mental health issues.

How does the individual friendship impact you on a personal level—in heart, mind, body, and soul? Note examples for each person listed.

Heart: How are feelings affected or changed?

Mind: How are thoughts and ideas altered or changed?

Body: How is physical health or daily activities/choices affected?

Soul: How are spiritual beliefs and faith challenged or altered?

What differences stand out between your lists? In what areas do you feel the greatest negative impacts? As this helps you see your friendships more realistically, begin to set goals for self-care specific to the areas of your life impacted in negative ways. For example:

Soul: "I will make it a habit to pray before and after encounters with this difficult situation. I will hand it over to God, when I have done only what I can, knowing there is much I cannot control."

Heart: "I will spend time journaling through the feelings I have in reaction to the difficult friendship. I will find a support person to talk to about my feelings."

Mind: "I will spend more time playing board games with my children to think about something else and worry less. I will read a book to learn more about the issues I have questions about."

Body: "To refresh myself after a time of helping, I will take a warm bath after I work out. I will sleep in tomorrow or I will go out and play today."

Questions for further reflection

1. Consider these, noting a specific person and circumstance. Revisit these questions in the future to appreciate your growth and change, or that of a friend.

- Seeing the negative effects of a friend's life situation on you, what might you decide to do differently next time?

In what situations were boundaries crossed or completely missing?

- What boundaries can you put in place to minimize the negative impact?
- What limits can you set that you haven't yet?
- In each circumstance, what have you learned about the way you handled each situation?
- In each circumstance, what new insights have you learned about yourself?
- What have you learned about the way you choose friends?
- What will you remember next time?
- In what ways have you grown through seeing a friend's negative situation?

2. Map Your Boundaries: Who, What, Where, When, and Why.

Where do you draw the line? Some women find it easier to begin this exercise by thinking about their children, or a child with whom they have contact. The idea of boundaries and limits might feel more natural when applying it to a parenting role. How would you firmly and kindly express loving and respectful boundaries and limits with a child you love? With this in mind, fill in the open ended phrases below. Next, repeat the same exercise with the boundaries and limits you want to put in place within a high maintenance friendship:

This is who I will set kind but firm boundaries with....
This is what I will do/support....
This is what I won't do/support....
This is where I will go....
This is where I won't go....
This is when I will help....
This is when I won't help....
This is how I will support/help....
This is how I won't support/help....
This is why it's important....

3. A Letter to My Friend's Addiction:

If you have a friend struggling with an addiction or unhealthy behavior, write a letter to it. Describe what you see, how you feel about the problem and how it impacts your friendship with this person. Share the note with your friend, or save it for your own personal reasons. A sample letter follows with open-ended statements to help you get started.

Dear Alcohol,

I know how much Mary loves you and needs you right now. I think she believes she can't live without you. She's afraid of life without you in it. You have come between Mary and me, and I need to let you know how you have changed and hurt our friendship.

I'm afraid of you because....

I am sad about....

I feel....

I am most confused about....

You have taken away....

I've noticed....

I want her to....

I want to help by....

I want her to remember....

I love her because....

God has already....

He also promises to....

Chapter 5

You

> My parents were abusive. Their hurtful words and actions are like a shadow that I can't shake; it follows me everywhere. Intellectually, I know I'm not to blame, but emotionally I'm still filled with a sense of worthlessness. I want to like myself when I look in the mirror, but I don't. I never feel good enough. *—Liza (age 44)*

Women are wonderfully complex, and every area of life experience—past and present—influences self-esteem. Former first lady, Eleanor Roosevelt said, "Friendship with oneself is all important, because without it one cannot be friends with anyone else in the world."

In order to be a friend to others, it's critical to learn how to befriend yourself and genuinely like whom you are meant to be. If you don't, the former first lady is probably right; you aren't likely to have many close friends.

Many aspects of American society detrimentally influence the growing self-recrimination many women experience today. Media messages portray unrealistic and even dangerous standards for women. Dogmatic religious doctrine can instill false beliefs and hopelessness, and all forms of childhood abuse or marital abuse can significantly alter self-image. For some, low self-worth, even to the degree of self-hatred, augments women's challenges in every facet of life. Whatever the source, actions and behaviors of women who dislike themselves scream out, "I hate myself," and shadow joyful relationships with feelings of unworthiness.

When you learn to appreciate and love the person God made you to be, including every aspect of your past and present life, a Christ-centered focus can help you and your friendships grow and develop in healthy, meaningful ways. Learning how to accept and love yourself is not to be confused with self-idolatry, so evident in the "me generation" of today. Self-examination can lead to a self-centered, selfish focus that promotes the idea that it's important to love your "inner goddess." If this happens, you end up idolizing yourself and have stepped away from the Christ-centered approach illustrated in this chapter.

When you see your reflection in the mirror, do you accept how you look on the outside—your physical self? Though it is important to accept and be satisfied with how you look on the outside, a "beautiful you" is realized by trusting that your beauty shines from the inside out—it's there you are anchored and strongly rooted—not in the outer layer of yourself that you see reflected in the mirror.

In the opening quote, Liza acknowledges self-acceptance is not always easy. A negative view of yourself can be like poison when it infects your beliefs about who you are and the kind of friend you can be. Learning to like the person you see in the mirror is a challenge many women face, regardless of age, profession, social class, economic, or marital status. However, you are ever-changing, and in faith, you can experience the acceptance and love for yourself that you may never have experienced or thought possible before.

The damaging words and actions of others may have

chained you to a negative self-image, but as you learn how to befriend yourself, the baggage you've carried from past experiences can begin to lift. Equally important, when you befriend yourself, you draw closer to God.

When It's Hard To Like Yourself

In an ideal world where babies are properly cared for and loved, the enchantment of a developing personality emerges day-by-day. In a nurturing environment where babies feel cherished and special, they bond to their mother and father, and in time, others. Soon children are fascinated and delighted to recognize their face in a mirror. It's only the beginning; positive self-worth is starting to form.

Women of every age wish they could consistently feel the way a well-loved toddler feels when she smiles at herself in a mirror—it's a need none of us outgrow. Scores of women would like to bottle a young child's innocence and unequivocal self-acceptance, because for many that disappears as they develop into adulthood.

Sue (age 36) said:

> I feel this sense of shame about myself, not just about my looks but about most everything. How I talk, what I say or think, even how I react to things. I'm always second guessing myself and afraid I'm going to stick out and embarrass myself. It gets so tiring. It's easier to be alone than try to socialize with people.

When it's hard to like yourself, it may be because undeserved shame has become an unpleasant appendage you've been forced to carry and accommodate. Undeserved shame is not a reflection of the person you really are, a reflection of something you have done, or something innately wrong with you. It's a lie, which over time becomes an ingrained belief. This fallacy is often the result of negative or harmful actions and opinions others have unjustifiably directed towards you. This form of shame has likely been falsely deposited within your heart, mind, and soul by someone else.

Lewis B. Smedes, author of the book, *Shame and Grace: Healing the Shame We Don't Deserve,* says, "In the past, I worried about complacent people who were blind to their own shortcomings. Now I worry about shamed people who are blind to their own strengths."

Natural shame, on the other hand, serves as a moral compass and is living proof of a conscience. When you learn from natural shame, integrity is built and character strengthened. Holding on tenaciously to either undeserved or natural shame can be detrimental to your well-being. It may foster feelings of inadequacy, guilt, and pain, all of which can destroy intimacy. Also, as you interact with friends and acquaintances, you may be perceived as unhappy, insecure, or too negative to be around. Carrying this kind of baggage into interactions with others leaves little room to experience carefree pleasure or close relationships with friends. James Joyce said, "Mistakes are portals of discovery." At this point it becomes critical to resolve guilt by learning how to forgive yourself for shortcomings and past mistakes, or perhaps for a history over which you had no control.

Be reminded of this message from Chapter One: Today, this very moment will never happen again, so if you need to make changes in how you feel about yourself, you can start right now.

Solutions

It truly is possible to learn to like the person you see in

the mirror, and once you've realized how to extend grace towards yourself, you may routinely find yourself offering it to others. Accept that what's true and good for others is just as relevant and applicable to you. Even though this change of attitude may not correct itself overnight, each day brings you new opportunity to imbed the love of God in your heart and mind. Slowly you will begin to recognize your own strengths and gain healthy respect for yourself, which will allow you to be a good friend and a happier, more confident woman. Remember: when you befriend yourself, you also befriend God. The outcome may surprise you.

In God's Own Image

In America, it's hard to ignore the youthful culture that surrounds daily life. Even women who recognize negative messages can't easily escape its influence. Technically perfected photos of women on magazine covers look real and have become a normal standard by which many measure themselves. They are a far cry from what's real. The commercial illusion of perfection so many people strive for has nothing to do with God's ideal for you. Diane (age 48) said:

> I hate the way young women are increasingly following the lead of the sex-driven media. Young girls look like "sex kittens" and seem desperate for this form of attention. It's not a healthy way for women to go through life. It drives me crazy! But even I can get sucked into it. The other day standing in line at the grocery store, I scanned the magazine covers and I honestly thought to myself, "Wow. I wish I looked like that!" I was in such a trance; the clerk had to yell at me twice to ask if I wanted paper or plastic! I was so embarrassed realizing even at my age I fall for it. It's ridiculous!

It's easy to ignore or lose sight of the perfect image God already provided for you, even though it's an image of great depth, not limited to what can be seen reflected in the mirror. Women can become easily distracted and "buy the lie" as they reach instead for an impossible standard.

Sandra (age 32) said this:

> Just one critical look in the mirror confirms the negative tape I have in my head about how ugly and disgusting my body is. I hate mirrors, cameras, even the reflection of myself in a store window. I hate my body and compare myself to every other woman in the room when I go anywhere—even when I'm among my friends.

Cultural lies can create significant shame and contribute to a distorted body image, threatening to squelch the spirit of a God who loves you just the way you are. Extreme religious conformists, those with legalistic and rigid views, can also attack your sense of worth and value.

Michelle (age 35) said:

> I grew up feeling dirty and bad. I could never measure up to my dad or to his expectations of me or his religious beliefs. I was told I was going to hell, that I was a sinner, and not good enough for anyone, especially not for God.

Legalistic conformists promote lies that bind as well as blind people. All too often, the message of a loving, accepting heavenly Father is lost at the hands of spiritually abusive, disturbed adults.

As Liza shares in the opening quote of this chapter, the physical and emotional abuse she suffered at the hands of trusted adults has followed her through life like a shadow. In some cases, women continue a path of self-destruction without knowing how to separate who they are from what has been done to them.

Marlene (age 40) was the victim of incest. She said:

> People think I'm happy and I probably look it, but the truth is I feel like I deserve the bad things I get. I've become promiscuous, and even worse, with the wrong kind of men. With each one, I'm digging myself in a deeper pit. I keep hoping one of these times someone will really love me. Meanwhile I go to church and I have some friends, but they have no idea who the real me is. I think I hide it pretty well.

Marlene may suffer in silence, but her feelings of shame and worthlessness aren't truly hidden. Her lack of self-worth is demonstrated in her sexual promiscuity and inability to open up about her feelings of undeserved shame with trusted friends. The relationship she holds with herself is self-sabotaging, because sadly, she feels she deserves nothing better.

Like so many women in similar situations, Marlene suffers behind a façade she presumes to hide behind. When women lose their freedom to be authentic and real, depression often results. Wearing a social mask to disguise true thoughts and feelings can be exhausting. Denying your true self is not honoring to you or God; it limits whom He intends you to be.

Some women continually "lower the bar" in relationship choices and give themselves away with the repeated false hope of attaining true love. Why? Because all human beings desperately need to be loved. Equating love with sex is a common mistake made by many women when they have been cheated of a healthy attachment and loving bond with an adult caretaker. They may have learned that sex pleases men, and men are whom they feel the need to please. This error in thinking triggers a chase for love and acceptance with a disappointing outcome, not unlike the dog who runs after an eluding tail, which always remains temptingly out of reach.

Mistakes are a part of life for everyone; so are poor choices and wrong decisions, though these vary in degree. Natural shame can create a profound sense of remorse and guilt that can linger much longer than you'd like. It's toxic waste to carry, so learning how to let go of past mistakes can help you improve your mental, emotional, physical, and spiritual health.

At the age of 40, Tammy knows from her own experience that beating yourself up does nothing to change a situation; it simply cuts you off from fruitful living. She said:

> I made a mistake I will always live to regret, and for years I believed I would never get past it. I beat myself up and felt I deserved all the guilt I could carry. But there's no going back no matter how much misery I wallow in. I have to remind myself that I didn't know then what I know now. I finally learned the best way to overcome a wrong decision was to move forward living right decisions—literally doing the next right thing! So that's what I'm doing now—doing the right thing whenever I can, and feeling really good about it. I'm done making myself pay; instead, I'm enjoying my life today and trusting God to continue teaching me how and why it's really okay to forgive myself. It's brought me a great sense of peace, and I've found the more I make the effort to help others with similar problems, the more I value myself.

What you can do:

• Highlight or place a checkmark on the points that are most true for you. Remind yourself of how every life experience has added depth and character to the person you are today. Revisit these on a regular basis as a way to gauge ongoing emotional and spiritual growth.

• Think about times when you've earned the experience of deserved shame. What did you learn? How did that experience change you?

• Give yourself permission to let go of past failures or choices you might regret. Make a list of these regrets and find a way to release them. As you burn, tear, or bury the list, offer it up to God to do away with guilt and self-revenge once and for all.

• Forgive yourself. Be loving and generous with yourself. Few women knew yesterday what they know today. You may not have had the maturity, wisdom, the set of circumstances, or character that enabled you to choose differently at the time. If you've accepted God's forgiveness, follow His lead and forgive yourself. Learn to cope with your mistakes. Expect to fail sometimes. Growth comes from learning to deal positively with mistakes and practicing self-forgiveness.

• When troubled by intrusive memories from the past, tell yourself, "That was then, this is now." Focus on the person you are today.

• Accept that everything in your past makes you the person you are today; all can be used for God's good purpose. Your life experiences—good and bad—give you the ability, empathy, and credibility to reach out and make a difference in the lives of others.

• Realize that to reject who you are is to reject God's own love and creation.

The deception imposed by a worldly culture, legalistic

religion, and abusive experiences are powerful, but they don't have to remain permanently entrenched in your soul. When you have a clear understanding of the source of your undeserved shame, you can begin to tear down the false messages behind it.

What you can do:

- Identify the sources of undeserved shame in your life. In what ways do you feel you can't or don't "measure up?" Write down the messages that have become ingrained from your culture, religion, or home. Do any of these messages demean, humiliate, or condemn you? If so, practice re-writing each message in a positive, accurate way, as if you were an objective observer of your situation. Say what you would have your best friend, child, or other loved one say to themselves in the same situation in order to correct and counteract false information.
- When negative feelings of deficiency, worthlessness, or guilt creep into your thoughts, stop them by visualizing a big red stop sign. Immediately re-focus on your strengths and personal gifts. Repeat this every time you catch yourself making a disparaging remark about yourself, either out loud or privately in your thoughts. Negative beliefs attack your self-image, feelings, spirit, and ultimately produce negative actions and behaviors.
- Remember the big red "Stop!"

Everyone asks at one time or another, "Why me? Why did this unfair and cruel thing have to happen to me?" Unfortunately, there is no pat answer or complete human understanding for some events. Sometimes the best explanation is simply that you were in the right place at the wrong time. Pain and suffering are a part of the human experience. Instead of asking "Why me?" try replacing it with the statement, "Why not me? Everyone has a cross to bear. I'm not the only one."

- Don't allow yourself to take the blame for other people's negative actions or feelings.
- Commit to rid your heart and mind of labels another person, or persons, has placed on you that has left you feeling less than you know you can be.
- Change can happen, and growth is an option that is a deliberate and daily choice.
- Don't get stuck in shame. Both natural and undeserved shame should have a time limit. Set an expiration date on shame, and then let it go when it's the appropriate time.
- Remember, you are designed in God's image, not any false one to which you may be clinging.

Let God Transform You

Lack of self love, for whatever reason, can be linked to friendship challenges. When a woman doesn't like herself, it can be revealed subtly through actions of criticism, distrust, animosity, self-doubt, competition, isolation, pretense, or aloofness. On the other hand, poor self-image is often exposed in more obvious ways. Some women over-compensate for perceived weaknesses by portraying a perfect life or sense of superiority over others. For example, women may project a sense of importance by reminding others of how busy and over-booked their schedule is. In conversations with others, some women may make it a point to drop names and information that help them look good or impressive, while others may continually put themselves down so no one else can.

Lack of self-love may also be acted out through moral choices like dishonesty, promiscuity, or abuse of others.

Inner layers of shame may affect and alter the quality of relationships and the ability to give as well as receive love. In whatever way it becomes evident, the negative feelings a woman has about herself are likely to result in actions that disrupt not only normal life, but in finding and keeping friends.

At the age of 31, Ellie still struggles with a negative self-image. She said:

> As a child the few friends I had always seemed to move away. I looked forward to high school to make more friends, but then when I developed health problems, my attendance was sporadic and I missed out on everyday academics and activities. When I was able to be there, I was ignored; I always felt like the new kid in school. I struggled to fit in, but people were cruel and excluded me time and time again. I tried so hard to be friendly and accepting of everyone else, but the continual disappointment of rejection was painful and upsetting. I felt something was wrong and unlovable about me, but for the life of me I didn't know what. I sank into a deep depression. I'm still sensitive to being excluded or left out in groups; that painful memory never goes away, even though I can see now it wasn't about me.
>
> Today I work with developmentally disabled adults, probably because I know how it feels to be ignored. My experiences of rejection have filled me with compassion for those who don't fit into the mainstream. Now it feels good to have the chance to help others feel accepted and respected, because it's the right thing to do.

Jesus provides examples time and time again of the importance of living a selfless life of service. By cultivating a servant's heart, you gain a healthy and secure sense of self in the process. Philippians 2:3-4 states, "Let nothing be done through selfish ambition or conceit, but in lowliness of mind let each esteem others better than himself [herself]. Let each of you look out not only for his [her] own interests, but also for the interests of others" (NKJV).

Becoming your best by accepting yourself, loving yourself, and growing a healthy sense of self-worth broadens character and moral fiber. Serving others becomes effortless, and unexpected blessings are sure to follow.

Whether your childhood was blissful or miserable, you were created with a wealth of goodness and gifts within you. Those don't go away; but as you heal, gifts are mined and rediscovered. Recognizing the tremendous possibilities within you is the image of yourself that God intends for you to see. He intends you to mine all the potential within you. When you make the decision to let God transform you, a new confidence can take hold, and your life and friendships can take a dramatic and positive turn. More importantly, you can find peace, joy, and a sense of purpose that may have eluded you in the past.

The ability to love yourself must be tenderly cultivated. With the personal desire and willingness to do so, it becomes an ongoing process of growth that continues throughout everyone's life. Henri J.M. Nouwen emphasizes this extraordinary love throughout his book, *The Return of the Prodigal Son:*

> People who have come to know the joy of God do not deny the darkness, but they choose not to live in it. They claim that the light that shines in the darkness can be trusted more than the darkness itself, and that a little bit of light can dispel a lot of darkness.

> They point each other to flashes of light here and there, and remind each other that they reveal the hidden but real presence of God. They discover that there are people who heal each other's wounds, forgive each other's offenses, share their possessions, foster the spirit of community, celebrate the gifts they have received, and live in constant anticipation of the full manifestation of God's glory.

> Every moment of each day I have the chance to choose between cynicism and joy. Every thought I have can be cynical or joyful. Every word I speak can be cynical or joyful. Every action can be cynical or joyful. Increasingly I am aware of all these possible choices, and increasingly I discover that every choice for joy in turn reveals more joy and offers more reason to make life a true celebration in the house of the Father.

What you can do:

• Highlight or place a checkmark on the points that are most true for you. Remind yourself of all that is positive about yourself and revisit these on a regular basis.

• Accept and remember you are no less valuable than any other woman. You have purpose and meaning regardless of the circumstances you have grown up in or experienced.

Make a list of your strengths, abilities, talents, and personal qualities you would not change. Ask three people who love you to add to your list.

• Be your own person. Trust your feelings, intuitions, and needs at any given moment. It's okay to have them, it's okay to listen to them, and it's okay to act on them. As Shakespeare's classic line states, "To thine own self be true."

Learn to accept your strengths and weaknesses, and never expect perfection from yourself. That is an integral part of self-acceptance, which is a critical factor to increasing self-worth.

• Seek out interesting friends with high self-regard and esteem. Let their positive attitude influence your own. Avoid people who make you unhappy or treat themselves or others disrespectfully.

• Accept you will not like everybody, nor will all like you. Your self-worth is not dependent on whether others respond positively to you or agree with you.

• Focus on your own growth without comparing yourself to others. Let any improvements you make be good enough.

• Boost your self-esteem by taking on new challenges that will stretch your abilities and help you grow. Remain flexible and open to new opportunities. Remember, both failure and success bring growth.

• Set realistic, attainable goals for yourself. Write down steps you need to take in order to achieve them. Be patient and persevere. Work on one small step at a time and take pride in every accomplishment, no matter how small.

• When having difficulty with goals, stay in this very moment; maintain a thought or change until the next hour, then commit to make it to the next day, month, or year. Celebrate your success, or if need be, commit to start again.

• Don't confuse self-idolatry for Christ-centered acceptance. Be mindful of the difference. Self-idolatry promotes a selfish attitude. A Christ-centered approach is humble and promotes the willingness and desire to serve others. Remember too much worldly self-examination can distract you from your relationship with God. Seek a balanced perspective.

• Do considerate things for others; it will help you feel

good about yourself. Greet each day with an attitude of service, directed towards others. It's as simple as giving someone a break in traffic, holding a door open for a stranger, or smiling at a store clerk.

- Make an effort to view others more positively. If you judge, criticize, and complain about others, you may be trying to compensate for your own low self-worth. Make the choice to change your interactions with others to improve your relationships.
- Give yourself the benefit of the doubt. Build on your strengths in your relationships with friends and minimize your weaknesses. If you find yourself talking about your weaknesses, choose to quietly reassess and work towards change.
- Use your spiritual gifts. Living a life for God is an investment; it will benefit others and yourself. Allow yourself to be vulnerable and truthful. In this manner, you will please God, and helping others will naturally follow.
- Look in the mirror and smile like you already love yourself. Even if you don't feel it yet, pretend that you do.
- Look in the mirror and tell yourself, "I love me the way God loves me." Even if you don't believe it yet, look yourself in the eye and say it out loud with certainty.
- Realize you can love the woman God made you to be—yourself.

When To Seek Further Help

No matter what issues might be interfering with the feelings you have about yourself, it can be helpful to seek out a trained professional to help you make progress with improving your self-esteem and sense of worth. Continually strive to keep a healthy balance of human and spiritual counsel, because both serve a valuable purpose to help healing and growth.

You can benefit from having someone listen, encourage, and guide you as you learn to overcome negative influences in your life. If you are the victim of a traumatic life event, or any form of abuse past or present, the impact on your feelings about yourself can be especially complicated and confusing. Make the decision to seek professional help to enable you to sort through the myriad of effects negative experiences have had on your personality and relationships.

If you repeatedly suffer from negative self-talk and beliefs or feel unable to express your true thoughts and feelings with others, seek the assistance of a counselor who can help you begin to discover all you are, and who you are meant to be. A trusted, knowledgeable counselor or therapist can support your journey to psychological health, which in turn can lead to greater physical, emotional, and spiritual wellness. If you experience persistent distress that prevents you from living your best each day, seek further help.

Behavior Checklist:

- Self-hatred or disgust
- A sense of chronic shame or guilt
- Sexual difficulties or concerns
- Low self-worth and feelings of failure
- Negative self-talk
- Negative beliefs about yourself
- Feeling cut off from your faith and relationship to God
- Negative feelings and beliefs about God
- Feeling fake or pretending with others
- Social anxiety, fear, or lack of confidence
- Extreme self-consciousness or embarrassment around others
- Poor self-image physically
- Never feeling good enough

Soul Solutions

> *You, O Lord, will not withhold Your compassion from me; Your lovingkindness and Your truth will continually preserve me* (Psalm 40:11).

Staying spiritually fit is a key aspect to recognizing self-worth and gaining self-acceptance. Through the eyes of God, you learn to see yourself as He sees you—your life is significant, and you can and do make a difference by being on this earth.

Within the love of God, as He gently reveals more of His character, you learn to love yourself. Through the compassion of God, you accept compassion for yourself, and through the forgiveness of God, the chains of unforgiveness that bind you are broken. Being sensitive to God's divine guidance can propel you to transform as you grow closer to the image He has of you. Through His eyes you will see an image that is deserving and worthy. And in time, you can extend the same generosity to others that God's given to you, bringing additional dimensions of joy and blessing to your life. Cynthia (age 46) said:

> Friendship has been a catalyst in my life. I would be a hopeless, self-centered, egocentric, tedious, arrogant, and probably perverse person if it weren't for honest friends who love me enough to keep me in line.

Eventually, or perhaps already, Cynthia may find herself helping others to stay in-line, as they desire to become the best they can be. When reciprocated and well-received, this is a great gift among friends who trust and love one another.

People are naturally attracted to positive characteristics,

strengths, and joy in friends. You can begin to exhibit these same traits when freed from the negatives that may have kept you from becoming your best. All the necessary ingredients to developing commendable characteristics and forming meaningful, trusted friendships can be found in a relationship with God.

God's free gift of grace promises to ease every burden, bring light to every dark corner, exposing and disposing the hidden shame that weigh so many down unnecessarily As you seek to grow closer to God, He can eliminate shame and break through self doubt and fear. Very likely, you have already tried numerous ways to escape undeserved shame, but holes of emptiness may still plague you. To feel accepted is an essential human need, but self-approval will not be able to penetrate your soul until the cycle of undeserved shame is broken. Trust that God's presence in your life can heal, and empty crevices can be filled with love, compassion, and forgiveness.

Claim and memorize this: God's grace replaces disgrace. Jesus said, "My grace is sufficient for you, for my power is perfected in weakness" (II Corinthians 12:9 NIV).

Julie (age 40) said,

> As a victim of sexual abuse, my soul was cold and guilt-ridden. I despised myself and didn't even know it since I'd always felt that way. I accepted Christ in my life, and now through healthy Christian mentors, I have learned to look to God to tell me who I truly am. I'm the daughter of a merciful, loving Lord. It hasn't happened overnight, but God has shown me that I am valuable and good, with many gifts to help others. I never knew life, or that I, for that matter, could feel this light-hearted and valuable.

Faith in God brings courageous confidence because you know you are not entering any day alone. Even if you are confused about how you see yourself, be content because you can patiently move forward in faith, day by day. God created you to be exactly who you are. Agree to progress towards becoming all of who He intends you to be and anticipate good things to follow. The undeniable therapeutic love of God can spiritually cure areas of darkness and pain.

Prayer Guide

As you turn to God in prayer, be reminded of how He will meet you right where you are as you face inner conflicts and challenges. He knows you—all of you. Close your eyes for a few minutes, and seek God and His loving-kindness. He is able, in ways the world and people are not always able, to help you overcome negative thoughts, feelings, attitudes, and beliefs about yourself. He restores feelings of self-worth and value like no other.

Instead of denying who God has made you to be, pray these words to God who loves you: "Search me, O God, and know my heart; try me and know my anxious thoughts; and see if there be any hurtful way in me, and lead me in the everlasting way" (Psalm 139:24).

Ask the Holy Spirit to be your helper in bringing you to wholeness. Ask Him absolutely anything and especially ask Him to heal the wounds that prevent you from being able to say "I love me" when you see yourself in the mirror. Cling to God's grace that removes disgrace. In humble silence before Him, allow God's acceptance to cleanse you from the previous shadows of humiliation or unacceptability. He already knows how you feel; He created you and will impart to you a refreshing hope that will soothe like a cool splash of water. God knows and loves you better than anyone, so tap into

His great resources. How gently He goes to those who are hurting. "You were tired out by the length of your road, yet you did not say, 'It is hopeless.' You found renewed strength, therefore you did not faint" (Isaiah 57:10).

What you can do:

- Depend on God; pray for guidance. A hopeful spirit can triumph. You are precious in His sight, and He longs to give you the desires of your heart.
- Know the Holy Spirit is ever-present to help you with any weakness.
- Serve others and unexpected blessings are sure to follow.
- Live with enthusiasm; expect blessings, and know goodness is meant for you too.
- Look in the mirror today and every tomorrow and say, "God loves me, and since He loves me, I also can learn to love me."
- What burdens weigh heavily on you and keep you downhearted? Talk or write about them in a letter to God.
- If shame is due to the words and actions of others, pray for guidance whether further help is needed. Ask God for His help to heal and forgive, and if needed, seek a reputable therapist.
- Pray to be restored to a true perception of yourself in the image of God, not relying on someone else's image of you or acceptance of you.
- Pray and read God's Word. In turn, you'll be shown more of the wonder of you.
- Through the Holy Spirit, God's unconditional love is with you every day. You are never alone. He promises to show you great things.
- Today accept that you are valuable. "Coming to Him as

to a living stone which has been rejected by men, but is choice and precious in the sight of God" (I Peter 2:4).

• Today know from whom you came. "Look to me, you who pursue righteousness, who seek the Lord. Look to the rock from which you were hewn and to the quarry from which you were dug" (Isaiah 51:1-2).

• Today know God is your protector. "Every word of God is tested; He is a shield to those who take refuge in Him" (Proverbs 30:5).

• Spending time with God, in prayer and His Word, will enlighten you much more than any words written on this page. May you find His goodness plentiful within yourself today.

Closing Scripture

Each week consider one verse you want to put into action and attitude. Take note of how these critical qualities make a difference in your relationships.

> *But you are a chosen race, a royal priesthood, a holy nation, a people for God's own possession, so that you may proclaim the excellencies of Him who has called you out of darkness into His marvelous light* (1 Peter 2:9).

> *For I am confident of this very thing, but He who began a good work in you will perfect it until the day of Jesus Christ* (Philippians 1:6).

> *Cleanse me from secret faults* (Psalm 19:12 NKJV).

> *Fix your thoughts on what is true and honorable and right. Think about things that are pure and lovely and admirable. Think about things that are excellent and worthy of praise* (Philippians 4:8 NLT).

Love the Lord your God with all your heart and with all your soul and with all your strength (Deuteronomy 6:5 NIV).

He restores my soul. He guides me in paths of righteousness for His name's sake (Psalm 23:3 NIV).

Look to the LORD and his strength; seek his face always (I Chronicles 16:11 NIV).

Do not be afraid for your Father has been pleased to give you the kingdom (Luke 12:32 NIV).

Do you not know that your body is a temple of the Holy Spirit, who is in you, whom you have received from God? (I Corinthians 6:19 NIV).

He heals the brokenhearted and binds up their wounds. Answer me, O Lord, for Your loving kindness is good; according to the greatness of Your compassion, turn to me, and do not hide Your face from Your servant, for I am in distress; answer me quickly. Oh draw near to my soul and redeem it; ransom me because of my enemies! You know my reproach and my shame and my dishonor; all my adversaries are before you (Psalm 147:3,16,19).

Friend-to-Friend Activities

1. Stepping Outside Yourself

Giving and serving others does the heart good and helps you feel satisfied and purposeful. It's a way to build self-esteem and character. Consider becoming a volunteer in an area of interest. New passion and enthusiasm for a worthy cause can bring fresh determination as well as enjoyment when you join friends with common interests.

You might also find ways to serve others as needs arise among women that you know. It's one of the most effective ways to grow as a Christian and focus on matters outside yourself. In the process you strengthen self-esteem by contributing to your sense of value and meaning, bringing you more to give in your relationships with friends. What's pleasing to the Lord will ultimately benefit you.

2. Personalize John 3:16-17 (TLB)

Change this verse to read with "I" and "me" to serve as a reminder that you can love yourself, because God first loved you: For God loved [ME] so much that he gave his only Son so that [I] who believes in him shall not perish but have eternal life. God did not send his Son into the world to condemn [me], but to save [me].

Remember—you are so important to Him that He gave his life for you. This is the living reality of Jesus—the Son of God—who experienced life as a man, died and rose, and whose loving sacrifice enables the Holy Spirit to intercede for each and every one who places their belief in Him.

Chapter 6

Relationships

> Because I've been in ministry for so long, I have friends who want me to wear a certain hat or play a certain role as their teacher, boss, or church leader. Some expect me to be a good Christian woman all the time. I am all those things, but not all the time! I have days when I fail miserably at living up to such roles, and the last thing I need is to feel I can't truly be myself with others. It's rare I find a friend that can accept all of who I am—including the flawed parts of myself. I want the freedom to be me, without editing. —*Amy (age 45)*

All women deserve to live a life that is real and authentic. Not only is it important for sound mental health and happiness in life, but the freedom to be genuine and "unedited" is the bedrock of every celebrated friendship.

Few movies portray the dynamics of women's relationships better than the 1989 comedy-drama, *Steel Magnolias,* written by Robert Harling. It is not a true story, yet it is. It portrays a bittersweet view of the realities of human relationships shared by a close-knit group of southern women in Louisiana.

Many women liked the movie because they could easily relate to the ups and downs of daily life the character's experienced. Movie goers also felt akin to the humor and heartbreak that impacted the flawed relationships depicted in the story. In the end the personal qualities of the characters helped them bond, survive, and accept their individual shortcomings. Scenes throughout the movie showed the circle of friends in disagreements over frivolous things, even though they never stopped genuinely caring for one another. They rarely censored themselves, and they found ways to be real with one another in nearly every situation they faced. Just like the characters in this movie did, women can pull together not only in the best of times, but even in the worst of times, and find agreement and acceptance for one another when certain qualities in their relationships are in place.

Whether it's a marriage, a work or sports team, friendship, or a family, the way you relate to others can bring accord or discord. Effective interpersonal skills are vital to any relationship, but all the skills in the world won't help a friendship lacking godly qualities. The ability to demonstrate unconditional regard and acceptance, effective listening, understanding, empathetic attitudes, and honest responses are vital to healthy relationships.

Successful women incorporate a number of these characteristics that lay the foundation for mutual growth and love in friendships. If you're like most, it's easy to lose sight of God's model for relationships. Character traits such as loyalty, trust, self-control, unselfishness, service, or respect can be lost through a damaging deed or a slip of the tongue.

In clear view, and given free rein, God's approach will never disappoint; it will give rise to harmony, making it truly possible to experience the best of relationships with friends. When God is the source of thoughts, actions, and responses, His love can be shared with friends through words and positive actions. Kindness, favors, and encouragement are a few of the tangible ways women demonstrate the love of God to one another. The qualities you contribute to friends is what makes your relationships flourish.

The Stages of Friendship: Sharing Your True Self

Henry Churchill King said, "So far as I can see the basis of friendship must be four-fold; integrity; breadth and depth of personality; some deep community of interests, mutual self-revelation and answering trust; and mutual self-giving."

Most women's relationships are developed in four general friendship stages. While many women acknowledge these stages, not everyone goes through them all or feels they fit their particular situations. As you think about the stages, keep in mind there or no right or wrong ways to move through them. Also recognize that not everyone will relate to this model of friendship development or find it true for their own experiences.

Women who relate to these stages describe themselves moving through them at varying speeds and at different times. Friendships can continue from stage to stage, or come to an end at any point along the way. The qualities present between friends at each stage of development seem to determine how relationships progress.

The first stage of friendship begins with a *connection,* a moment when women feel drawn to certain characteristics or interests in one another. They may click instantly, or sense there is a possibility of a good friendship with this person. Women often describe feeling a sense of euphoria and excitement at this stage because they've met a new friend who seems to have a real connection with them.

The second stage of friendship consists of an interval of

time when *learning* takes place. During this period, continued and important discoveries are made about one another. This is the stage where friends really get to know each other on a broader, less superficial scale. They are introduced to deeper parts of one another, and emotional intimacy is beginning to form. The strength of the felt connection often determines how personal and quickly emotional intimacy develops. At this stage many women say they feel blessed and thankful for having this new friend enter their lives. A sense of worth is evident between them.

The third stage of friendship consists of *challenges* to the relationship, as outlined in the first several chapters of this book. The manner in which challenges are faced and resolved often determine whether or not the friendship moves forward. Those that continue, gain a new sense of gratitude for the relationship's resiliency and staying power.

Finally, the fourth stage of friendship consists of genuine *love and care* in the relationship. At this point some women say they've even found a soul mate. From here, the relationship continues to grow, change, and unwrap like a gift over time and through every stage of life.

Sometimes women move from stage one to stage four in just one short meeting. Cyndi (age 48) said:

> When I met my best friend, we both knew instantly we were going to be soul mates. We connected immediately in a deep and real place, as if we'd already known each other forever. Everything about her told me she and I were meant to be friends for life. We still look back and smile on that day, because we knew we'd be standing here 25 years later still feeling grateful for our relationship and still feeling excited that we met.

Many relationships don't happen the way Cyndi's did. Women also say good relationships have evolved and deepened for them more slowly over time. A sense of history between friends can move a relationship across the stages in an unhurried but no less meaningful way. And for some women, the stages present a considerable personal challenge; it's not always easy to share intimately with others.

Women who struggle to share with others on deeper levels often aren't comfortable revealing intimate parts of themselves. Some avoid, hide, or attempt to camouflage feelings of inadequacy by assuming a counterfeit persona. This habit is often driven by a fear of not measuring up. Some women adopt images to stand behind in an attempt to find validation and acceptance. The need to appear perfect, important, highly educated, blameless, smart, or religiously virtuous may leave powerful impressions on others. The need to portray an image of "supermom," "scholar," "perfect wife and homemaker," "righteous and religious believer," or perhaps environmentally "pure" are also ways of saying "I have it all in control" and perhaps, "I'm doing this better than you."

Of course, true intimacy in friendship is often formed at times when life feels out of control and women don't have it all together. These are the vulnerable, shaky periods women walk through, when they need support and understanding from friends who encourage them to be open and honest. Most importantly, women need someone they can be completely real with, exposing their true selves—uncensored. Lee (age 52) said:

> I can tell you the exact moment when I knew Reana was a true friend. I let my guard down completely one day and told her the truth about my life. My husband never went to church, we separated for a time,

> my daughter was involved in sex, alcohol, and had legal problems, and I had just suffered the loss of one of the most important positions I had ever held in my career. I felt like my years of education and the status I held were a complete fraud. Basically, she met me when my world caved in and I was experiencing the worst stress of my life. And guess what? When I poured all this out, she didn't bat an eye. She shared similar struggles she had overcome, some of them identical to mine! She totally understood and accepted me, warts and all. It took our friendship to another level—one of total trust.

Another way to live a pretend life or deny your true self is to suppress and bury authentic thoughts and feelings in order to please, protect, or appease others. It's a hard thing to suppress one's true nature and life experiences. It's a process of perpetually burying parts of the self and denying their existence. In some cases, women simply don't know how to allow their true selves to be known. For others, the mere thought of being completely transparent creates anxiety, which is more comfortable to avoid. In either case, many women have been well-trained by others to ignore their own sincere reactions and deny the core of who they are.

Fear of intimacy can inhibit relationships and so can the fear of not measuring up. Women who deny their true selves are likely to suffer from more depression, anxiety, and stress than those who don't. Putting on a front and holding on to artificial images can be like an unwieldy millstone around a woman's neck. When the true self is deeply and thoroughly hidden, it often leads to profound loss and sadness.

To be yourself in a truly authentic and honest fashion can be risky. However, in most friendship situations, revealing inner thoughts and feelings is an important and healthy risk to take. How can you really get to know someone? Go beyond the superficial and be fully known and understood. Being yourself is necessary to grow deep and lasting friendships and definitely the only way to gain a soul mate. God made you to be who you are in relationship with others. Letting your personal light shine in all interactions is a worthwhile goal.

Solutions

At times it is an act of courage to live boldly and to be the person God made you to be. Friends can foster honesty between one another by following God's approach to relationships. When you practice "The Pearls of Wisdom," you have the opportunity to model God's love in action. The pearls consist of: **P**atience, **E**ncouragement, **A**cceptance, **R**espect, **L**oyalty and **L**aughter, and finally, **S**ervice.

The art of effective and godly communication provides the strand that runs through each pearl, intertwining them together ensuring a beautiful necklace is created—a relationship formed. Bringing your best self to every relationship happens every time you choose to display your pearls and impart their inherent priceless qualities.

The Art of Communication

Most women love to talk, especially to one another. They usually believe they hold all the communication skills they'll ever need. For the most part, upon further examination of what women say, why they say it, and when, they acknowledge some challenges in at least a few areas. Learning to speak your truth in the right way and listen in a way that sincerely hears, are qualities on which every solid friendship depends.

Saying What You Mean and Meaning What You Say

Speaking truth sometimes separates you from others in a way that is painful and isolating. When what you say causes you to stand alone, it's especially difficult. Jody (age 34) said:

> When I was the only person with a particular opinion among my friends, I used to feel like I was back in high school. My insecurities surfaced, and I braced myself for criticism and rejection. It was hard, but I finally learned it was worth it for me to speak truthfully, even if it didn't make me popular. After all, I am an adult now! I feel like some of these friends are beginning to respect me more for standing up for what I believe, so it's been a good change in me.

God understands the challenge of standing alone only too well and in fact prepares us for this experience. As Christians, believers are called to be different, and in many cases this should give cause for celebration. Jesus said that making the decision to follow Him would mean divisions in relationships. Not everyone will accept or appreciate the path of a Christian. In the same way, saying what you honestly mean is not always easy, so clearly communicating and courageously standing by what you say is crucial.

What you can do:

- Pray for guidance in everything you share in relationships.
- Give thought to all you want to say before you speak. Consider your tone and body language, because they can speak louder than words.
- Take your time and identify what you truly think and

feel. Sit on it awhile. don't speak until you are sure.

- Rehearse what you want to say, and keep it simple.
- Consider how you expect to feel one day later, two weeks later, or six months down the road after speaking your heart and mind.
- How will relationships improve by your choice to honestly express yourself? What is your desired outcome?

Trust is critical in any relationship committed to open and honest sharing. Feeling safe to disclose secret parts of yourself is an essential first step. Building trust is a process involving time and experience, but there are ways to develop it sooner rather than later. Where there is maturity and perseverance, there will ultimately be a deepening sense of mutual trust in relationships.

What you can do:

- Follow through with what you say you will do.
- Keep others' private information private.
- Keep your word; be dependable.
- There's nothing worse than sharing a confidence only to have it used against you or condemned. Commit to a nonjudgmental position and avoid criticism that will only serve to break apart a relationship.
- Practice effective listening as outlined below.

Listening So That You Hear

Henry David Thoreau said, "It takes two to speak truth—one to speak and another to hear." Because of its great value, listening is another powerful gift friends give to one another. When you show the ability to listen carefully to others, you communicate far more than words can express. Listening tells a friend, "I'm putting you first because I care about you." Allowing friends to vent helps lighten whatever burdens they may be carrying. It also tells them, "I want to know you and understand who you are, unedited." The simple act of careful, deliberate listening also helps establish a sense of empathy. To help you discover and really understand the depths of a friend's point of view and life experience, empathy is essential. Acceptance is built when you learn to choose to see the world as your friend does. Respect in relationships is born out of empathy. Psalm 17:6 directs us to listen: "Incline your ear to me, hear my speech."

What you can do:

- Choose to take the time to really hear others as you listen to them.
- Learn to listen with an ear of love, respect, and acceptance. Listen with your heart.
- Make the choice to view situations and experiences from your friend's perspective, experiences, and world view, rather than limiting it only to your own.
- As you listen, ask questions to clarify and verify what you hear to be certain you are accurately and fully understanding.
- Relax when you listen so you can take in everything that is said without distraction.
- Whether on the phone or in person, avoid doing other things while you are listening at the same time. Give your full attention to what is being said so friends feel valued and know they are your priority.
- Model the way you listen after someone who listens well to you.

What to avoid

- Pay attention to times you interrupt another person.

Apologize out loud and tell yourself to stop when you are tempted to interrupt again.

- Don't jump ahead and reach your own conclusions; let friends finish talking, completely.
- Avoid making assumptions or adding your own spin regarding others' lives.
- Fight the urge to speak over someone else while they're still talking. This cuts them off and devalues them. You communicate disregard for what someone is expressing and ultimately this breaks trust.
- Break the habit of finishing other people's sentences for them, even if you're certain what they are about to say. You're wrong more often than you think, and you're guaranteed to miss a lot when you take over the conversation. You rob them of the opportunity to speak their own mind.

Practicing the Pearls of Wisdom: Actions and Attitudes to Wear Every Day

Relationships are continually shifting and being redefined. At the core of every important and meaningful friendship is a close relationship that adjusts and compensates as needed. In order to stay healthy, relationships require plenty of attention and commitment. The following pearls are the qualities that can strengthen relationships and help realize their potential. Wear these actions and attitudes every day to help your friendships remain dynamic and growing.

Patience

As 1 Corinthians 13:4 reminds us that love is patient and kind. It bears all things. Patience, when put into action, can be a tremendous present to give a friend. It proves that you care for them through thick and thin. Patience shows you can let something irritating slide off, as you choose to forget or forgive. It also gives you the perseverance to come alongside a friend who may have long-term problems, complaints, or pain.

Patience, when materialized in human form, is seen as even-tempered, caring and diligent. It brings composure and stability to the smallest inconveniences and strengthens togetherness during trying circumstances. Women who are able to personify patience bring expressions of kindness and wisdom that touch gently and humbly. In the words of Vauvenargues, "Patience is the art of hoping."

Encouragement

Even a spark of encouragement given to a discouraged friend can rekindle hope and soothe the spirit. In Romans 1:11-12 Paul told believers that he wanted to see them so they could encourage each other. He says, "I long to see you . . . that I may be encouraged together with you while among you, each of us by the other's faith, both yours and mine."

For believers, sharing the bond of Christ can be especially powerful. The strength of encouraging words between friends should not be underestimated. In mere seconds, they can uplift and inspire.

Kathi (age 55) wrote this note to her friend:

> Your friendship has been a catalyst in my life. When we are together, I come away with renewed vision and energy to reach beyond where I am and follow my dreams. Thank you for that! There is something about our being together that thrusts me forward—it is true! Isn't that what a part of friendship is all about?

Positive, healthy relationships lead women to courageously do things they yearn to do. They don't demand approval or damage one another through rejection and critical judgment. Supportive relationships encourage you to examine yourself to determine how best to grow your special gifts and God-given talents. Through these types of relationships, their usefulness to God is expanded.

Acceptance

Unconditional love and acceptance are qualities Christians are called to demonstrate, just as Christ did in His relationships. All relationships that remain close and stand the test of time understand the absolute grace and mercy that's contained in them.

In describing the most important blessing friendship has provided, Mary (age 54) said: "To be fully known and still loved and accepted! That is the closest to being like God that one person can be towards another. To be given that from a friend is huge and freeing."

Felicia (age 35) added, "Having someone who knows you well enough and loves you well enough to gently point out your blind spots but at the same time puts up with your faults—that's mercy in action."

Loving unconditionally means you believe in and respond to the best in a friend, regardless of her mistakes and weaknesses. It does not mean you accept sin or turn a blind eye towards it. Loving unconditionally means you care enough about someone to love them even when it's challenging, and at times, undeserved.

Hosea 3:1 says it best: "Love a woman who … is an adulteress, even as the Lord loves the Sons of Israel." Just as God continues to love, so should you.

Marita (age 44) said: "The greatest blessing of friendship is this: Love. I am not alone."

If your friend has a loving heart, she has something of God in her; put aside her shortcomings and embrace what's heavenly in her.

Respect

Respect and integrity go hand in hand. It takes integrity to balance between giving good counsel to friends or being too blunt and hurtful. You want to share enough, but not too much. It takes integrity to walk this fine line in the right way. Respect allows you to forge the appropriate way to share and interact in healthy relationships.

When an attitude of respect exists, it builds confidence between friends. It also bestows high esteem and regard for friends' opinions and feedback. Jill (age 28) said: Respect means there is truthfulness, reliability, and honor in my friendships, and it brings with it certain rights and privileges. My friends can say nearly anything to me, if I know they respect me."

Loyalty

Loyal friends remain devoted and trustworthy. This valuable quality among friends must be mutually earned and does take time to develop. A loyal friend's actions stand out; they are faithful and steadfast regardless of what might or might not be occurring in life. When others walk out, a loyal friend steps in. Faithful friends are unwavering, even in the face of anger, upset, competition, betrayal, and loss.

Jennifer (age 47) said:

> My marriage came undone after my husband repeatedly broke my trust and left me for another woman. I never knew how important my friends were to me until I went through this. They were the only loyal relationships I had left; they literally kept me alive.

They were constant companions when I couldn't be alone, and they remained true and faithful friends when I had no one else to turn to. They reminded me there was still plenty to love about myself. If that's not loyalty, I don't know what is."

Laughter

The character, Truvy, played by Dolly Parton in *Steel Magnolias* said, "Laughter through tears is my favorite emotion." If laughter could be prescribed in daily doses like medicine, everyone would be healthier. Proverbs 15:15 states, "He who is of a merry heart has a continual feast." Relationships that share a strong sense of humor, no matter how far-out or whacky it seems, tend to grow into fast friendships and enjoy a continual feast.

Laughter allows for an instant joining between friends and a natural sense of camaraderie. To know you aren't alone in your thoughts, feelings, and unique or quirky perspectives is powerful. Without laughter, a part of friendship remains untapped and unknown. Humor drives relationships deeper in a non-threatening and pleasurable way, and it's good for the heart, mind, body, and soul.

Kaye (age 68) said this about the relationship she has with her friend:

> Anything that makes us feel we are the funniest women that ever lived, with hours of giggle fits to prove it, is what's so priceless about our relationship. Our extensive history of 'inside' jokes is like an unwritten testament of our life and crazy times together."

Anya (age 29) shared this example of a message she sent to her best friend, knowing full well she would appreciate the humor and sarcasm as much as she did:

> Are you tired of those sissy friendship poems that always sound good, but never actually come close to reality? Well, here is the stone cold truth of our friendship. When you are sad, absolutely doooooo cry into your beer. And be sure to wear black and pout! You should be totally EMO (emotional and grumpy). Oh, and write bad poetry. Be sure to use the word "crimson" in there somewhere, then we'll go egg someone's house, and get tattooed and pierced. Love, Anya.

Most women agree: more than anything, it's the fun they have together that makes a friendship work. Fun and laughter grow a relationship the way the right soil and the correct amount of sunlight brings a seed to life.

Service

An undeniable quality to any relationship is the ability to serve one another in times of need. Debora (age 51) wrote:

> I sprained my ankle the day before my parents were coming to town. A close friend of mine knew I was in a jam. Not only did I need to pick them up from the airport, I had grocery shopping to do and the house to clean. In no time, she was there for me, reporting for duty! I can't tell you how relieved I felt to have her there for me. Through this I came to appreciate knowing that in a serious family crisis, I won't be alone.

The give and take between friends needs to be balanced. When friends consider themselves equals, this is a natural outcome. But some women find it difficult to be on the receiving end of help. They may find it tough to relinquish control, believing someone's help proves they have a weakness or fault, or they feel too self-conscious to accept the attention given them. When you only give to others and never allow others to serve you, the relationship cannot expand and grow as it naturally might. Eventually the friendship loses important vitality and strength, which are important ingredients for lasting relationships.

A thriving friendship can't help but produce good works, and in doing so strengthens bonds. Service between friends can extend well beyond meeting the needs of one another and branch out to meet the needs of your community or a common cause you both support. A relationship that serves together can't help but reap all the rewards of giving together, and what a gift you will enjoy as you watch blessings overflow to others.

Relationships With Benefits to Both

When positive qualities are strong in relationships, many women say spending time with a best friend is the greatest therapy in the world. Friendships that are working well share similar qualities to a positive therapeutic relationship. There is trust, sharing of wisdom, examining the depths of the soul, kindness, mercy, patience, acceptance, honesty, integrity, encouragement, respect, counsel, teaching, foresight, service, humor, and unconditional love. When a number of these qualities are present, along with a strong commitment to do the work, a gratifying and rewarding sense of harmony can be developed and enjoyed.

When To Seek Further Help

Relationships are important in your life, so if you struggle persistently with any of the following challenges, seek out support for help with developing important relationship skills and qualities:

- Unwillingness or inability to express honest thoughts and feelings
- Chronic or frequent impatience towards others
- Critical or judgmental attitudes
- Need to compete with friends, rather than encourage them
- Find it difficult to balance an equal give and take in relationships
- Find it challenging to guard personal information and/or refrain from sharing confidences
- Find it difficult to follow through with promises
- Resent or feel pressured to be of service to friends

Soul Solutions

God shows women how to be in honorable relationships with friends, and the only way to maintain a godly level of friendship is to obediently seek Him on a regular basis. Communication is polluted by the world, but God's Word gives a fresh and accurate perspective to life with motivation and guidance that is undisputable.

In I Thessalonians 4:9, Paul writes:

> *Now as to the love of the brethren, you have no need for anyone to write you, for you yourselves are taught by God how to love one another.*

God is a living conduit for teaching how to effectively

communicate in relationships. His loving and wise guidelines are clear and provide a perfect resource for all people. His examples demonstrate the qualities that result in solid friendships, grounded in mutual growth and love. As the only perfect guide and model, God can help you create pleasing harmony in all relationships.

Prayer Guide

As you turn to God in prayer, be reminded of how He will meet you right where you are as you face challenges in your past, present, or future relationships with friends. Close your eyes for a few minutes, and seek God and His loving-kindness. Trust that He has your best interests at heart. Know He will help you bring out the qualities in your relationships that bring mutual love, joy, and support to your friendships.

Ask God to help you live your life in a way that is agreeable to Him, knowing His way is what makes relationships work. Be thankful for the model He has provided you as well as the unconditional love and acceptance that is always there for you. Ask for strength and courage to be able to express your true self in every relationship, even when you may be set apart from others for your actions, beliefs, or ideas. He can help you learn to say what you mean, and mean what you say. Welcome Him inside your heart, mind, and soul to be the source of your thoughts, conversations, actions, and responses. Then all your relationships will grow in mutually caring ways and according to His plan.

What you can do:

- Ask God to bring His perspective and clarity of words to your communications.
- Seek maturity in faith; through the Holy Spirit ask for

help in keeping pride, harsh opinions, or any unkind or callous words and actions from your relationships with friends.

• Pray to be worthy of your walk with the Lord by demonstrating His love to friends; exhibit the love of God in all you say and do.

• Ask God to bring friends into your life who will exhibit an equal and corresponding level of trust.

• Remember the power of God transforms people through His love. If there is a personal need in your relationships with friends, pray because God is the perfect listener.

Closing Scripture

Each week consider one verse you want to put into action and attitude. Take note of how these critical qualities make a difference in your relationships.

> *Love one another* (John 15:17).

> *And so I am giving a new commandment to you now—love each other just as much as I love you. Your strong love for each other will prove to the world that you are my disciples* (John 14:34-35)

> *Dear friends, let us practice loving each other, for love comes from God and those who are loving and kind show that they are the children of God, and that they are getting to know him better* (1 John 4:7 TLB).

> *May God who gives patience, steadiness, and encouragement help you to live in complete harmony with each other—each with the attitude of Christ toward the other* (Romans 15:5 TLB).

> *Two are better than one, because they have a good*

reward for their labor. For if they fall, one will lift up his companion (Ecclesiastes 4:9-10 NKJV).

A true friend is always loyal, and a brother [sister] *is born to help in time of need* (Proverbs 17:17 TLB).

You have no right to criticize your brother or look down on him. Remember, each of us will stand personally before the Judgment Seat of God (Romans 14:10 TLB).

Let's please the other fellow, not ourselves, and do what is for his good and thus build him up in the Lord (Romans 15:1-2 TLB).

Don't be selfish; don't live to make a good impression on others. Be humble, thinking of others as better than yourself. Don't just think about your own affairs, but be interested in others, too, and in what they are doing (Philippians 2:3-4 TLB).

Friend-to-Friend Activities

1. Meet My True Self

Take your time, in one sitting or over several days, to make a list of important aspects regarding yourself and share them with a friend. Include the following:

- a secret
- a time when you were at a crossroad in your faith
- two dreams
- a deep hurt
- your greatest regret
- best memory
- two faults
- two mistakes
- the focus of your last prayer

- your deepest reason for gratitude
- your worst fear
- your greatest weakness
- your greatest strength
- something about yourself you would change if you could
- an experience you would change from your past if you could do it over

Share as much from your list as you feel comfortable. Together, discuss what you have learned from this exercise about yourself and about one another.

2. Encouragement Note

Surprise a friend with a word of encouragement. Mail her a note, deliver it to her work, or place it on her porch with a favorite book, magazine, or flower from your garden.

3. Service Project

Individual: Find three ways this week to serve your friend. Mail her a book you've wanted to share, pick up her children from school, pray for her, e-mail her scriptures to inspire and encourage her, take her out to coffee, spend more time listening, or help her with a dreaded task.

Community: Plan an activity together where you serve others in your community or support a cause about which you both feel passion. Research your program or organization of interest and inquire about how to best help or volunteer, utilizing each of your individual talents and resources. Once you've begun a project, consider the mutual rewards gained through your philanthropy. Look for unexpected blessings that may occur, mutually and individually, as you generously give of your gifts and time.

PART TWO:

FRIENDSHIP AND BEYOND

Chapter 7

Finding Friends

> The next best thing to being wise oneself is to live in a circle of those who are. —*C.S. Lewis*

Surrounding yourself with perceptive, strong, and understanding women is a wonderful goal, but finding a wise circle of friends isn't always easy. Even finding one good friend can be a challenge sometimes.

Many women grow to depend on the strength, wisdom, and insight they draw from one another. They know life can be rich and satisfying in the company of close and trusted friends; personal growth and contentment can't help but blossom.

However, not everyone is equipped to make friends easily, and not everyone necessarily wants to either. Some women confess that they "don't get along well with other women," or complain, "there aren't many good friends out there." Others simply leave it to fate, believing if it's meant to be, they'll become friends by happenstance.

Of course, most friends don't fall out of the clear blue sky and drop conveniently in front of you. Some level of effort and connection has to happen in order to bring someone into relationship with you, even when the circumstances of your meeting seem amazingly serendipitous.

You *can* learn how to step out of your comfort zone, change ingrained ideas and assumptions about people, and make new social connections happen. Like so many other endeavors, finding friends often requires you to take an active role in the outcome. Be willing to revive your personal efforts towards meeting new women.

Your challenge is to find opportunities to become acquainted with more people and then to seek those select friends with whom you can share your deepest thoughts and feelings—authentic expressions from the heart, mind, and soul.

Fortunately, finding friends—whether casual or intimate—is not dependent on perfect social skills, status, popularity, or good luck. Of course, being friendly and outgoing helps, but what seems to matter most is the readiness to be yourself, unedited, and your willingness to look for what's authentic and good in the people around you. Divine intervention certainly helps, and so do godly qualities, but authentic effort and interactions will go a long way in the search to find friends.

The key to finding friends rests on your ability to step outside yourself and appreciate what is truly interesting and loving in another person. When you take the time to notice valued friendship qualities in someone you meet, you have nearly found a new friend. Simply put, *the art to finding friends is discovering how to recognize them.*

Keep the following suggestions in mind as you face new opportunities to seek out friends. It's important not to limit yourself to only certain groups or types of people. Keep in mind that doorways to new friendships are all around you. Learning to recognize them is your first goal.

What you can do:

• Make it your mission to get to know the people around you. Show a genuine interest in what others say and what they think and feel. Learn what's most important to them in life.

• Be a good and sincere listener, practice empathy, and encourage others to tell you about themselves. For example, "Tell me what happened...that must have been a really hard time in your life... how did you get through what you did...I admire your attitude and the way you handled it...."

• Make it a habit to be interested in the talents, gifts, and skills of others. Explore all the unique and rich sides to each person you meet. Pay attention to strengths. Set a goal of understanding what makes a person special and original. Encourage and support their accomplishments.

• Being authentic means being the same person in public as you are in private. Strive to be the kind of person people can trust. That means speaking up and saying what's true for you too.

• Keep any personal insecurity you may have in check, otherwise you may come across as too needy or not genuine. For example, in an effort to hide flaws, some people inflate their egos and exhibit a "better than thou" attitude towards others. Displaying a sense of arrogance is the quickest way to turn potential friends away from you.

• Healthy self-confidence and a positive self-image make it easier for people to approach and feel comfortable around you. It can't be faked, but it can be developed and nurtured. Seek the help of a professional counselor if you struggle with a lack of confidence or low self-esteem.

• A sense of humor and the ability to laugh at yourself shows you can accept your own imperfections and still have fun. Most people are drawn to fun-loving people. When you don't take yourself too seriously, others will probably want to be around you more.

• Pursue common interests you share with others once you've discovered them. It's mutually beneficial, fun, and a great way to grow a closer friendship.

• Expose yourself to new possibilities and opportunities whenever you can. Olympic skater, Sasha Cohen said, "If you do what you've always done, you'll get what you've always gotten." Try new groups, clubs, classes, or activities that peak your interest.

• Show people that you sincerely like them. It's easy to forget to tell others how much you enjoy, love, appreciate, or respect who they are. Let people know exactly how you feel. Show them they matter to you.

• Spend more time doing and less time worrying about finding friends. Focus on being positive, warm, and cheerful. It's the best way to attract new friends—a smile goes a long way.

• Partner with God to help you find friends. Remember to pray and make your requests known. God already knows what you need and cares about what you want. Trust Him to bring about social contacts that are right for you in His time frame, not yours.

• Focus more on being a friend rather than having friends. J.R. Miller said that to be a friend, "is the life of Christ in the soul."

Imperfect and "Out of the Box"

A Turkish proverb wisely states, "Who seeks a faultless friend, rests friendless." You will never find a friend without imperfections. Let go of any fantasies you might have of finding an ideal or perfect friend. Even the best of friends cannot be in complete harmony all the time. No one is flawless. Everyone has frailties, and if you're seeking friends without a few shortcomings, you'll always be disappointed. Don't sabotage your efforts to recognize potential friends by holding unrealistic expectations. Imperfect friendships are still better than perfect loneliness. "Two are better than one." (Ecclesiastes 4:9)

This viewpoint can also help to broaden your ideas of where you can find friends. Rosa (age 34) said:

> When I first joined my church I was exposed to new people in classes and study groups that I would never have bothered to get to know otherwise. Our differences were obvious, and our personalities completely different. But I can't tell you how much these people have enriched my life just by knowing them. And to think I almost missed out on not having them in my life! It pays to put yourself out there, even among people that you think you have nothing in common with. Friends can be found everywhere we find ourselves.

Make an effort to step outside the box. You might even find the adventure of "trying on" new types of friendships to be fun and exciting. Don't confine yourself to one type of personality or person who is comfortable for you to be around. Relationships fill many purposes and offer assorted ways of adding enjoyment to life, so be open to the variety of possibilities. Try not to gravitate exclusively to those women who share your same age, ethnicity, or lifestyle. Don't shy away from someone's talents, skills, or political and religious viewpoints just because you don't understand them. Philip Yancey offers this insight, "I am drawn to friends for different reasons. With some I share common values and interest, but I also enjoy eccentric friends who encourage me to see things unconventionally. In either case I look for someone who will reward my honesty and not punish it, who will push my introverted self to a deeper level of intimacy" (*Prayer*, p. 59).

Like day and night, different types of people are needed to make the world go 'round. A mixture of friends expand your horizons and challenge you to grow in previously untapped directions. Everyone has the potential to contribute to your personal growth, maturity, and wisdom. Let them!

Closing Poem

The following poem expresses the joy and appreciation for all friends found, and for those special few who mean everything to you.

Friends I've Found

I've found friends at different times
Who gave me strength and pleasure.
And I've found friends in different climes
Who gave me thoughts to treasure.
I've found friends in strange, strange places
I never dreamed they'd be.
I've found friends with bright, clear faces
Who lit fires inside of me.
I've found friends who leaned on me
And let me be the "strong" one.
And I've found friends who let me lean
And let me be the "wrong" one.
I've found friends who saw my best
And encouraged me to grow.
And I've found friends who saw the rest
And knew growth might be slow.
But you, dear one, were all these friends

Which sets you so apart.
And you, my friend, will always have
A place within my heart.
—Kathryn Wilson

Chapter 8

Growing a Relationship with God

> I made one decent choice that has affected my life more profoundly than all my poor ones combined: I chose to believe Jesus. —Beth Moore, from *Jesus the One and Only*

There is no other friendship that will satisfy the way a relationship with God can. Still, you are given free will to be involved or connected with whomever you choose. God invites you into relationship with Him, but He's not going to force you to receive what He has to give. He respects human freedom and lets everyone decide if, when, and how they will come into relationship with Him.

But how do you grow a relationship with God? And how in the world can you have a relationship when there's no face-to-face dialogue, lunch meetings, phone calls, or communication with a person you can actually see? How do you make a relationship real with God?

God wants all people to come to know Him. He established the opportunity when He brought His Son into this world. Through Christ's life and death, you are given a personal view of God's all-encompassing love, grace, truth, and forgiveness. Your worthiness to know God rests on Christ, not on good works, respectability, or righteousness. When you learn about Christ, recognize and accept who He is, and invite Him into your heart, you begin a journey with a new friend and Savior. Christians will tell you: The ordinary becomes extraordinary when you accept Jesus Christ and experience His faithfulness.

Still, there are as many different relationships with God as there are believers. He meets each person wherever they are in their journey to know Him. Your kinship with God is as unique as He made you. And yet, the miracle of the Holy Spirit reaches down to personally touch each person's circumstances, no matter how desperate or depraved. It's beyond human understanding to grasp, but the change in a person's life is not. It is profound and ongoing. God is authentic.

Though all people are imperfect, the impact of even one believer's life on others can make a dramatic and positive difference in the world, one person at a time. This is one more reason to nurture your relationship with God, to learn more of who Jesus is, and to recognize how the Holy Spirit helps you know Him. But a friendship with God takes courage. You are called to be "different" in a world full of opposition to Him. You are asked to trust and believe on faith alone, and walk on "the road less traveled." This chapter is for anyone who wishes to begin, renew, or deepen a relationship with God, the Author of our faith.

Prayer: The Ultimate Art of Communication

A relationship with the Almighty encompasses the same level of communication you enjoy and depend on with a true and trusted friend. It takes an intentional connection with God, a persistent act of communicating, to awaken you to His presence. Anyone can invite God into their life and bring their life into God's presence through the simple act of prayer.

Whether you are aware of it or not, you already have

God's full attention and commitment. In His presence you can feel safe. And in order to grow closer to Him, you only have to make room, let Him in, and allow His Spirit to live through you.

In most intimate relationships, when you speak to a best friend, you can skip the small talk and go straight to the heart of what matters most. So it is with God. Prayer allows you to expose your true self and speak your truth with blistering honesty. Like authentic friendships, prayer offers you the chance to be loved in whatever state you happen to be in at any point in time.

Mother Teresa said, "If you want to pray better, you must pray more." So keep talking to God. Make your requests known. Communicate with Him in any form you want—through words, writing, song, silence, meditating on Scripture in any way that comes natural and is comfortable to you.

If you have stopped praying for any reason, and feel cut off from your relationship with God, simply begin praying again. The only mistake you can make is to never go back to talking to God!

What else you can do:

• Remember, all growing relationships take time. Be patient. Finding quiet time with God might be a challenge, but keep Him company on a regular basis. Even though He is ever-present, if you neglect to communicate through praying, listening, and continually learning, His influence on your life is minimized.

• Create a healthy devotional life balanced on prayer, worship, reading His Word, and a mutual sharing of faith with others. Begin by reading Psalms to discover all the different levels of friendship available to you with God.

• In his book, *Prayer,* Philip Yancey writes, "We can invite God into our lives and ourselves into God's. When we do that, putting ourselves on a personal footing with God, so to speak, relationship heats up and a potential for extraordinary friendship stirs to life. For God is a Person, too, and though a person unlike ourselves, One who surely fulfills more of what that word means, not less" (p.62).

What If I Have Doubts?—A Walk in Israel

Unless you are one of the fortunate people born with the gift of faith, it's natural to doubt, question, and consider intellectual logic over faith. You may be a person who has had a past experience of losing faith in God, or you may be living in that time now. You might be reading this today and not know Him at all, or have so many questions it seems impossible to accept what you read here. It's okay. Be assured—you are loved. He patiently waits for you to seek a relationship with Him, a gift freely given.

Imagine for a minute, a time warp. You find yourself in Israel during the years when Jesus lived and walked there—you're standing in a crowd. You have the privilege of observing the woman who had a flow of blood for twelve years, and you watch as she humbly comes from behind to touch the hem of Jesus garment, saying to herself, "If only I may touch His garment, I will be made well." He turns around, and seeing her says, "Be of good cheer, daughter; your faith has made you well." (Mark 5:34) You are awestruck by His compassion; your heart realizes He is able.

From there, you are suddenly standing next to the Sea of Galilee; you smell the water, hear gentle waves lapping on the shore, and with bare feet you step into the cold sea water. As you walk along the shore, you see Jesus beckoning Peter and Andrew to follow Him (Matthew 4:18-20).

Suddenly Jesus turns, and seeing you, says the same thing, "Follow Me." Even from a distance, you feel His presence—warm and assuring as you stand in awe, hardly noticing your cold, wet feet.

As you imagine yourself in this time frame, personally follow His actions and your reactions. Are you drawn to walk up and talk with Him? Imagine how it would feel to look directly into His eyes as He says, "I am the bread of life" (John 6:35), "I am the light of the world" (John 8:12), "I am the resurrection and the life" (John11:25). And as He speaks these words, imagine Him suddenly reaching out to place His hand on your head. *Imagine!*

Gratefully, we do not need to be in Israel in that day and time to rest in His presence. Through the Holy Spirit His love, grace, and peace can touch you just as clearly as the words on this page, but don't stop here.

What you can do:

- By developing friendships with other believers, you can help strengthen your Christian walk. But most importantly, rely on God to give you spiritual perspective and guidance as you seek it. He both comforts and convicts, fairly, promoting inner growth that will allow you to do and be much more than seems possible.
- Find a trusted church to teach, mentor, and pray with you. Surrounding yourself in the fellowship of other believers inspires and strengthens.
- Find quiet time to slowly read (and perhaps re-read) the gospels that tell Jesus' story. Let the passages of Matthew, Mark, Luke, and John resonate in your life. Recount His words and actions, and ask yourself how they affect you and your life story—your circumstances, your hopes, and your dreams. Know that He is "able to keep you from stumbling,

and to make you stand in the presence of His glory blameless with great joy" (Jude 24).

• See the examples of the ways Jesus connected and valued people from every walk of life. His priorities included acknowledging, touching, socializing, empathizing, listening, teaching, and loving others. You will grow in your relationship with God as you grow more like Him. And His presence in you is magnified when you treat others according to His example. Expect more of God's character to root deep within you, bringing faith, change, hope, and healing.

• Frequently highlight or journal scripture that is significant to your current circumstances. How can you apply this scripture's teaching to your daily life? How has reading it made you different? Conclude by writing a brief prayer of request and thanksgiving. Get in this wonderful habit as you read throughout the Bible. Try these suggestions as well:

• Note which circumstance or person you closely relate to in Scripture. Why?

• You have the written gift of history in the Bible. Individuals described in its pages were real people who are valuable models and mentors today. What does their example teach you? What scripture brings you comfort, reminding you that you are not alone?

• What verse(s) stand out as evidence of His presence in your life today?

In Relationship with God, You're Never Alone

Everyone feels emotionally alone sometimes. However, spiritually you are never alone. Don't rely on emotional feelings. Accept the simplicity and freedom that is in God in Christ. The key is to regularly choose to participate in a relationship with Him, desiring to travel this life with Him at your side, not because you have to, but because you can't imagine life without Him.

A sincere yearning for more will take place, and you'll understand a whole new love language deep within your spirit. Walk with Him, talk with Him, and welcome His living water to quench whatever causes you to thirst, offering up yourself to His plan and purpose for your life. In your spiritual walk and lifelong process of growth, there is always more. Look forward, walk on. With Him, you have a very reliable best friend, mentor and encourager, listener and leader.

As you strive to accept all God has to offer, leave yesterday behind, and have confidence in today and tomorrow. In your imagined visit to Israel, dip into the Jordan River. Be baptized in your belief in Jesus—in Him you are made whole.

Closing Scripture

Thankfully, Christ's example and story is one that is written down in the Bible. Being the Word of God, it allows the Holy Spirit to minister personally to you. It is undeniably the best guidebook for life that's ever been written. No one will ever arrive and have it all together in this life, but thankfully God does. Through scripture, He equips you as you choose to follow Jesus' footsteps in your life-long challenges and in your process of growing closer to Him.

How does it make you feel when He speaks these words from John 15:11-15?

> *These things I have spoken to you so that My joy may be in you, and that your joy may be made full. This is My commandment, that you love one another, just as I have loved you. Greater love has no one than this, that one lay down his life for his*

friends. You are My friends if you do what I command you. No longer do I call you slaves, for the slave does not know what his master is doing; but I have called you friends, for all things that I have heard from My Father I have made known to you.

Mapping Exercise

Stones to Recognize and Commemorate Your Spiritual Journey:

Each of the 12 tribes of Israel took one stone from the riverbed of the Jordan and stacked them together to commemorate their exodus from Egyptian captivity and the crossing into God's promised land. This served as an historical marker of what God had done for them (Joshua 4:1-8).

Think about the path of faith you've walked throughout your lifetime. As demonstrated in the example on page 199, begin by drawing one horizontal line on a blank piece of paper—continue with as many lines as needed in order to map out the following:

1. On your personal time line, chronologically list ages you were when significant events took place that influenced your faith journey both positively, and negatively.
2. Below the time line: List those events, life circumstances, people, and other influences that negatively influenced your relationship with God. For example, list the struggles or times you turned away from God, experienced personal doubt, crises, or rebellion. It may include periods of time where you gave up on faith completely, or felt numb to it.
3. Above the time-line: List significant events, life circumstances, people, and other influences that have positively influenced your relationship with God. These may include spiritual and life experiences that made God real for you, inspired your faith, brought your beliefs into focus, and brought strength, hope and growth.

Let this written recognition of your journey, your stones, be a reminder to commemorate where you've come from and where you want to go. You may be reminded of how clearly God has come into your life, and how easily you can be distracted and forget the evidence of His presence. This is also a wonderful record to share with friends, family, and children. It can help keep your relationship with Christ, real. Below is an example of a time line.

PIVOTAL EVENTS—Drew Closer to God

Young Child	Pre-Teen	Teen	Young Adult	30+	40+	50+	60+
Family & Church Baptized		Praying w/Abby Death		Received Christ! Bible Study		Phil. 4:13 Christian Friends	
		Too cool	Divorce Self-Reliance	Sick Fear		Who am I?	Lonely

PIVOTAL EVENTS—Drew Further From God

For You make him [her] *most blessed forever; You make him joyful with gladness in Your presence* (Psalm 21:6).

You are our letter, written in our hearts, known and read by all men; being manifested that you are a letter of Christ, cared for by us, written not with ink but with the Spirit of the living God, not on tablets of stone but on tablets of human hearts (2 Cor. 3:2-3).

For those who are according to the flesh set their minds on the things of the flesh, but those who are according to the Spirit, the things of the Spirit (Romans 8:5).

Chapter 9

Leaving a Legacy of Friendship

He who laughs, lasts! —Mary Pettibone Poole

Have you ever thought about what your friends will say about you when you're gone? It's a question most people wonder about at one time or another. It can certainly motivate you towards examining yourself and honestly assessing your words, actions, and the way you are demonstrating love for others during your lifetime.

It is a lifelong process, but a thrilling accomplishment if you are able to leave a legacy behind for others. To make a positive difference—no matter how small or large—is exciting and meaningful. A legacy is a personal gift, handed down from one generation to the next. Though material possessions can be a wonderful inheritance, giving of yourself has a "live" spark of remembrance that can span and influence generations to come. Legacies are priceless and ongoing.

Think About Your Legacy

What choices and actions can you take in order to leave a friendship legacy that flickers when you're gone? In the span of a lifetime friendships intertwine, reconnect, and weave anew. Lasting relationships are a direct result of women who demonstrate a spirit of giving and trustworthiness, while setting healthy boundaries for themselves.

Most women know what it means to give to others in tangible physical ways, but a giving friend does this emotionally and spiritually as well. For example, as a loyal and trustworthy friend, you keep confidences and have the courage to be lovingly honest in discussions and disagreements. You keep each other accountable to shared spiritual goals. There is no end to the laughter friends can share—or tears! You hold up one another in prayer, and most of all, you listen.

All behaviors and actions taken towards friends will leave their mark; none are easily erased by the washing of time. But it is how you made your friends feel that will ultimately determine how you will be remembered by them. There is a multitude of ways to ensure your legacy is one of which you will be proud.

What you can do:

- Be an honorable friend to all you meet.
- Let your words and actions say, "I value you."
- Trust others; be a friend others' trust.
- Freely share all you have to give. Put the gift of giving into action—yourself, skills, and resources. Reveal your dreams to one another, and then offer sincere encouragement and interest in a friend's goals—cheer her on!
- Reflect the goodness you see within your friends and raise the level of your own goodness at the same time.
- Be sensitive to pivotal life moments in the lives of your friends. Care!
- Honor a friend—share in her achievement and success with enthusiastic interest.
- Stand beside a friend who can carry a burden alone no longer.
- As friends, problem-solve and encourage one another—

offer your faith in God to give needed direction and personal support.

- As you seek to draw closer to God, and He reveals more of Himself to you, "your story will tell God's story," inspiring friends to live life with hope and promise.
- Make yourself memorable; a godly woman is never forgotten.
- Be loving and value people, just as God loves and values you.
- Listen, pray, love, offer reassurance and requested counsel—this is giving—this is building a legacy.

A Final "Friendship" Note

The most important message in this book bears repeating: Be authentic and intentional in your relationships with friends—enjoy today, this very moment, and live the life as the woman God made you to be. Remember to love (even when it's hard), learn (every day), laugh (even at yourself), and be thankful and content with what you've been given. You can't help but radiate warmth to those around you when your cup is filled with gratitude. This dear friends, will leave a lasting impression and an enduring legacy to all who know you and call you friend.

Closing Scripture

Now it came about when David had finished speaking to Saul, that the soul of Jonathan was knit to the soul of David (2 Samuel 18:1).

Final Friendship Exercises:

1. Draw a "Friendship Tree."

Make a sketch of your favorite tree with a big trunk and multiple branches. The trunk may be labeled with God, or anyone who has been a strong influence in your life. On each branch write one friend's name. At the end of each branch, write one word that describes her legacy to you. Pray over this "tree" with gratitude, recognizing each friend who is a significant and important part of your life story.

2. **Write your own legacy.** What will your friends say about you when you're gone? Write a letter about what you would like to hear about yourself through the eyes of your friends. How do you want to be remembered? Write down how your friends would describe you, what made you special, what qualities you shared, what you gave, who you loved, how you lived your life, and what was important to you.

Save this letter and read it periodically. It will serve as a reminder of what you need to do to ensure you leave the friendship legacy that is important to you. Nurture it!

3. **Write a legacy letter to a friend.** Write a letter as described above. It will be a priceless gift for someone special to you. Share it as a way to remind her of the value she holds to you and to everyone in her life.

May you practice the art of authentic friendship from this day forward...

It is never too late to be what you might have been.
—George Eliot

HELPLINES and RESOURCES

CRISIS SUPPORT

National Domestic Violence Hotline
1-800-799-7233 (1-800-799-SAFE) (24-hour bilingual) • TDD 1-800-787-3224
http://www.ndvh.org/

National Suicide Hot Line 1-800-273-TALK (8255)
American Foundation for Suicide Prevention www.afsp.org

National Institute of Mental Health 1-800-64-PANIC
http://www.nimh.nih.gov/

Sexual Abuse Hotline (sexual assault, incest)
1-800-656-4673 • http://www.rainn.org/ (rape, abuse, incest national network)

National Center for Victims of Crime
1-800-394-2255 (1-800-FYI-CALL) • (including abuse & domestic violence, rape)
TTY/TDD 1-800-211-7996 • http://www.ncvc.org/

Postpartum Support International 1-800.944.4PPD (4773)
Postpartum Depression (and Perinatal Mood Disorders)
Toll-free Help Line • http://www.postpartum.net

SELF HELP / SUPPORT GROUPS

NAMI (National Alliance for the Mentally Ill) • 1-800-1-800-950-6264
(1-800-950-NAMI (education and support for friends and family of mentally ill)
http://www.nami.org/

Hospice Foundation of America (Grief and Loss) 1-800-854-3402
(Helps to cope with terminal illness, death, and the process of bereavement)
www.hospicefoundation.org

The Compassionate Friends (Loss of a Child) 1-877-969-0010
Non-Profit, self-help support organization open to all bereaved parents, grandparents, and siblings.

ADDICTION

Alcohol-Drug Treatment Referrals National 1-800-996-3784 (1-888-996-DRUG)
(24 Hrs) • http://www.nationalhotline.org/ 1-888-762-3750 (1-888-SOBER.50)

findtreatment.samhsa.gov/ 1-800-662-4357 (1-800-662-HELP English and Español)

http://www.alcohol-drug-treatment.net/ 1-800-510-9050

Al-Anon (for friends and families of alcoholics) 1-800-356-9996
http://www.al-anon.alateen.org/
Meeting Information 1-888-425-2666 (1-888-4AL-ANON)

Comprehensive Addiction Programs Inc. www.helpfinders.com

Mothers Against Drunk Driving (MADD) 1-800-Get-MADD www.madd.org

National Council on Alcoholism and Drug Dependency Hopeline: 1-800-NCA-CALL

HEALTH

Anorexia Nervosa and Related Eating disorders Inc. www.anred.com

National Eating Disorder Association Helpline: 1-800-931-2237
http://www.nationaleatingdisorders.org

Eating Disorder Recovery www.edrecovery.com

Weight Watchers (Good eating choices, healthy habits, a supportive environment and exercise) • http://www.weightwatchers.com

TOPS Club, Inc. (Take Off Pounds Sensibly)1-800-932-8677 (1-800-YEA-TOPS) (support for those who want to take and keep off pounds sensibly).
TOPS Headquarters Phone: (414) 482-4620 • http://www.tops.org/

American Cancer Society 1-800·ACS·2345 (Meet other survivors, find or offer support on the Cancer Survivors Network. Find lodging, workshops, transportation, and other services and products) • http://www.cancer.org

Cancer Information Services 1-800-422-6237 • http://cis.nci.nih.gov/

About the Authors

Photography by Katelyn Alexander

From left: Debra Whiting Alexander and Judy Dippel

JUDY DIPPEL is a wife, mother, writer and speaker. Her first book, *Refreshing Hope in God* (WinePress), speaks compassionately to the hearts of mothers everywhere. Judy is currently writing a Bible Study on postpartum depression (Care-Point Ministry—2009).

Judy is a frequent luncheon, conference and retreat speaker. Like a close friend, her relaxed speaking style connects easily with her audiences. She says, "God's grace will never cease to amaze me—it's a privilege to share how our stories tell God's story."

Judy enjoys hiking and outdoor activities, college sports and golf. She feels learning something new and reading a good book are some things she strives to do every day. As a baby boomer, she appreciates the value and influence friends have on her life. She enjoys sharing with women the worth of all relationships including those with God, family, and friends.

If you are interested in inviting Judy to speak, please contact her directly through her e-mail address at JLDwrites@comcast.net or website, www.judydippel.com, or through any of the following speaker services: www.CLASServices.com, www.WomensMinistry.net and www.MinistryWomen.net.

DEBRA WHITING ALEXANDER, Ph.D., is a mental health practitioner and the author of more than sixteen published books including, *Loving Your Teenage Daughter (Whether She Likes it Or Not)*, *Children Changed by Trauma*, and *The Emotional Recovery Resource Kit*. She is also a contributor to *The One Year Life Verse Devotional* and served as consultant to the award-winning video series: *Saving Our Schools from Hate and Violence*.

In addition to her Ph.D. in Psychology, she holds a Marriage and Family Therapist License and is a Board Certified Expert in Traumatic Stress. Debra's career spans more than twenty-five years in California, New York, and Oregon where she provided a broad range of mental health services and was a frequent conference presenter. She also held positions as a Professor at both Northwest Christian University and Oregon State University.

Debra says, "One of the key's to good mental health is expressing gratitude for something everyday." She loves the ocean, reading fiction, and her baby grand piano. She enjoys hiking, camping with her husband and friends, and a good western. Debra currently is working on her first novel in Eugene, Oregon, where she lives with her husband of nearly twenty-five years and is the mother of one grown daughter and a twelve-year-old Golden Retriever.

To contact Debra, e-mail at: drdeba2003@yahoo.com